High Probability Options Trading

Jim D. Dawson

www.trade4profits.com

Facebook: www.facebook.com/Trade4Profits-1700359833625590

Twitter: trade4profits1

Copyright @ 2019

All Rights Reserved

ISBN: 9781798022832

TITLE: High Probability Options Trading

AUTHOR: Jim D. Dawson

PUBLISHER: J.D. Dawson

www.trade4profits.com

Facebook: www.facebook.com/Trade4Profits-1700359833625590/.com

Twitter: trade4profits1

Disclaimer

Trading involves risk. Trading options can substantially increase your risk. It is important that you clearly understand the risk involved in every trade. Sometimes you can lose more than you have invested with options. I am not a professional financial adviser, what I offer in this book is a brief description of what I have found successful. I do lose money on trades. This is not a book about 'how to get rich' trading stocks.

You should contact your financial adviser to help you understand your risk.

I am not suggesting that a specific strategy is appropriate for you, I only want to let you know some of the strategies I have found work for me. I trade a variety of strategies only some of which are in this book.

This book is for educational purposes only.

Preface

There are lot's of books out there about how to trade, some even written by me. But, there are not a lot of books that let you see the trades as you will see them when you are trading. Trading is about greed and fear. Fear of losing money and greed of making money. When you start to lose money you either say "I must get out now before I lose more" or even more dangerously "I must stay in until it turns around." When you are making money you must fight the desire to take a profit while you have it or the desire to make even more if you just wait.

Typically if you wait for it to turn around you lose more money. If you do not take profits, they have a habit of going away. That is why it is important to trade a trading plan. Know why you are getting into a trade, when you need to get out (or defend) and when you need to take profits (either full or partial). This is your trading plan. Always trade your plan, do not change it during the trade.

So, how do you know when to change your trading plan? First of all, as I said before, not during the trade. You refine your trading by keeping a trading journal. You review your old trades frequently. Identify what you did wrong and what you did right.

Some of the gross money received on my trades may seem low even though the return is good. Please keep in mind that most of these trades can be scaled up utilizing additional contracts/shares to bring in more gross money. One of the reasons I sometimes use less contracts is because of other positions I have open using the equity and/or margin in my account. I do not trade just one trade at a time, I usually have multiple positions open with varying expiration dates.

I debated about whether or not to show commissions in my trades. The problem is that although there will always be commissions they can vary greatly between accounts. I have trading accounts with four different brokers and all the commissions are different. I took a middle of the road approach and decided to show commissions on some trades but not on others. You can tell the ones that do not have commissions included by the total prices.

When describing the trades I am only using their stock symbol. It would be good for you to know what these stocks are in order to fully understand how they trade. Stocks, ETF's and Indexes behave differently and typically have different volatility and option prices.

I discuss this more in Trade4Profits – Shortcuts to Profitable Trading, if you have not read that book I highly recommend it. Yes, I could give you their names and describe them for you but trading takes work and this is part of that. You will remember them more if you look them up for yourself.

I would also recommend that if you have a charting program that will show you the period I am trading that you pull the charts up. That way you will be able to get a better idea what I was seeing while I was trading. Try not to look at what happened after my trade until you see why I entered when I did. Then scroll forward and see what I traded through.

I know some of my trades in the book appear differently in the way I account for buying and selling. The truth is, sometimes I go back and forth in the way I keep up with my positions. Seems like sometimes one way makes sense, the I decide another way of tracking the trades make more sense. I thought about standardizing my trades for the book but then decided not to. The whole idea of the book is for you to see what I was seeing and thinking during the trades. That includes not being able to make up my mind the best way to document them. Don't worry, it will not be difficult for you to follow. If it was unclear I put the profit or loss in a way easy to understand at the end.

These are not all of my trades during this time period, I skipped around some to make sure you got a good example of my trades and thinking. You will see gains and losses in the book. Overall, the percentage of gains and losses you see here are about the same if I included every trade I made.

If you are not an experienced trader (and even if you are) I urge you to paper trade before ever trading with real money. I also encourage you to use a good trade calculator to see where positions are profitable, where they are break even, what your total risk is and what is your maximum profit and where. Although I use a number of different brokers, TDAmeritrade has my favorite trade calculator.

This book has some of the same trades in you will see in my Trade4Profits Watch Me Trade books, the biggest difference in this book is that I am focusing on high probability option trades as opposed to everything I trade.

I also introduce our Strangle trade rules for the first time in one of my books. Strangles can be an important money maker for you but be careful not to over trade them because they have uncapped risk.

Typically we keep Strangles to about 10% of our portfolio. The worst thing that can happen is if you have a lot of initial success trading Strangles. When we first started trading Strangles we one our first 15 trades, only had to even adjust one. So, we increased the number of Strangles we had in our portfolio, looked like easy money.

Then, the market crashed. We got lucky and we did not hesitate to adjust and close our positions when necessary. We did lose money but it could have been a lot worse. Remember, every strategy has a weakness even if you have a 80% win rate.

The market always decides winners and losers and there is a loser for every winner. Don't over trade.

- Keep your portfolio balanced

- Don't enter all your trades the same day/week.

- Watch your portfolio delta. We don't get crazy when adjusting but we do keep in in mind when we place new trades.

- Don't over trade.

- Don't risk too much on any one trade. Most trades we do at 1% to 2% of our portfolio. Index Iron Condors are at about 5%.

POSITION SIZES: **One thing you will notice is I show 1 or 2 contracts a lot of the time. I do this for a couple of reasons. One is that I don't want you to focus on "I could have made xxxxx" I want you to focus on how these trades work. Another is to help keep my personal portfolio values confidential. I base my position sizes in my portfolio balance as compared to the risk in the position.**

Some of my older trades still show my original contracts, I did this to stay consistent with my original Watch Me Trade book. It was in Watch Me Trade 2 I started only showing 1 or 2 contracts instead of my actual contracts.

Table of Contents:

Chapter 1 – About Me

Chapter 2 – Iron Condors – Index

Chapter 3 – Iron Condors - Non-Index

Chapter 4 – Broken Wing Iron Condors

Chapter 5 – Butterflys

Chapter 6 - Strangles

Conclusion/Take Away/Risk Warning

Short hand used throughout the book:

BC: Buy to Close a new position.

BO: Buy to Open a new position.

C: Call Option.

CT: Contracts

GTC: Good to Cancel

P: Put Option.

SO: Sell to Open a new position.

SC: Sell to Close an open position.

Chapter 1

About Me

For those of you that read any of the Trade4Profits books you can skip this section. If you haven't read them we recommend you pick up Shortcuts to Profitable Trading especially if you are new to trading options. If you are an options expert, you probably don't need it.

Both of our Watch Me Trade books have many of the trades you will see in this book. There are also additional trades in them if you want to get an idea of everything we trade. We just wanted you to know there was some duplication.

I started trading in the early 90's. Back then information was hard to come by, especially if you were not in the industry. You also did not have sites like Amazon.com where you could easily search for books to read about stock trading and financial analysis. If you wanted to find a book about the stock market you had to go to the library and use the card catalog and find a book using the Dewey Decimal library classification system. Depending on your age you may not even know what I am talking about.

I had seen movies about the stock market and it looked exciting to me. I was confident that it was something I wanted to learn about and could eventually make money doing. My wife worked at a bank that had a securities department that would allow you to purchase stocks. Back then there were not really any discount brokers you either had to use a bank that offered the services or open an account with a major brokerage firm and pay their prices. Since I wanted to pick my own stocks I chose to go the banking route.

I still had the problem of picking what stocks to purchase. Finding out information back then about a specific stock was difficult. Everything wasn't at your fingertips like it is now. There were a few newsletters you could subscribe to if you could find them. You also had the Wall Street journal and your local newspaper which posted stock prices everyday. I am not even sure if they still do that, it has been so long since I have picked up a newspaper.

Not having much money back then I did not want to pay for a subscription to the Wall Street Journal so I would pick up one weekly at a local book store and attempt to educate myself on the markets. I would also examine the local newspaper trying to see some sort of pattern in the huge listing of companies and their relevant price information. Remember I also did not have access to all the free charting software and previous price information that we have access to today.

After a couple of months of trying to self educate with little or no experience or idea what I was doing I decided the best way to invest was by purchasing stocks that I heard something about and waiting for them to go up in value. Now that I had a system, such as it was, I had to pick the stocks. The best idea I came up with was if I saw a companies name then I could assume other people would see it and want to buy the stock.

The first stock I picked was a company with a local office. Everyday I drove by that office and made the determination that it must be a good company because it was on a main road, the office looked nice and a lot of people seemed to work there. The company's name was Unisys, stock symbol UIS. If I remember correctly they were trading at about $2.00 per share back then which was great for me since I did not have much money. I made the call to the broker at the bank I was using and bought about 300 shares.

The second stock I picked came to me as I was watching the Sugar Bowl. The Bowl game was being sponsored by USFG and I figured if they had enough money to sponsor a game of that magnitude they must be a good company to invest in. I also figured that since a lot of people were watching the game that others would feel like me and be purchasing the stock soon. I do not remember how many shares a bought but I felt good about my choice.

Now I had my funds invested and the waiting game ensued. I watched the stock prices religiously in the local newspaper. For the most part they stayed the same. I am convinced (although I have not researched) that stock prices moved much slower and trended better back then. Trading was a much more difficult process with large brokerage firms controlling all the action. Now not only can you trade much more easily as an individual than you could back then using online discount brokers you also must compete with computers trading billions of dollars themselves; I will discuss more of that later.

Eventually I sold those stocks after holding them over a year. I made a small amount of money on both of them but realized my dream of picking a stock and getting rich overnight might not be possible. There were a number of reasons I rationalized for that.

First, with the small amount of money I had to purchase a stock I would have to buy stocks prices at $.05 per share and hope they went up to $10.00 per share. That rarely happens and you are more likely to go broke than make any substantial money trading penny stocks. Do not fall victim to the mass emails taunting penny stocks. Can you get rich that way? Maybe. Will you? Probably not.

Second, I had no idea what I was doing. I knew I needed to learn more about trading and figure out the best stocks to purchase. I needed a plan. That is when I started my education in earnest. I became an avid reader of all books about the market.

Over the years I have studied buy and hold, covered calls, options, trend following, too many day trading strategies to list, turtle trading, Elliott Wave, seasonality, candle stick trading, chart pattern trading and too many other things I have probably forgotten myself.

As I write this I look around my library and can see well over one hundred books, that does not include some that are probably still in the garage in boxes from my last move. I have also spent thousands of dollars on trading classes for currency, futures, options and stock trading.

The bottom line is there is A LOT of information out there and you can become lost in the desire to learn. Information paralysis is a real thing. Eventually (by the early 2000's) I decided options were the best way for me to take advantage of my limited funds and use other strategies I like to pick the stocks.

During that time period online trading was becoming available, access to online data about stocks and free charting was becoming readily available which really kick started my ability to successfully trade.

Just in case you do not know what an option is I will briefly talk about them. My trading is heavily reliant on them so you must understand them. If you still do not understand them after you read this book I suggest you search online until you are 100% familiar with them and their uses. Keep in mind you must always understand the risks with an option.

You could lose more than you have invested if you trade higher risk strategies.

A couple of definitions before we start:

Option – right to buy or sell a stock at a specific strike.

Strike – the price which a stock can be purchase or sold.

Call – the right to buy a stock at a given price. You can sell a call also but ignore that for now.

Put – the right to sell a stock at a given price. You can sell a put also but ignore that for now.

Time Value – the amount of the options price that is based on how much time is left before the expiration of the option. Some options have just time value and other have both time and intrinsic value.

Intrinsic Value – the amount of the options price that represents 'in the money' value of the stock. If you purchase a Call option with a strike of $15.00 for $1.15 and the stock is currently trading at $15.50 then $.50 of the $1.15 option price is intrinsic value and $.65 ($1.15 - $.50) represents time value. If the option expires at exactly $15.50 then you option would still be worth $.50 but the time value of $.65 would be gone.

Basically a stock option is the right to buy (CALL) or sell (PUT) a stock at a specific price. Let's say GE is trading at $36.50 today and you believe it will go up but can't afford to purchase very many shares of GE at 36.50. If you wanted to purchase 200 shares that would cost you $7,300.00. You could purchase the right to buy GE at $36.50 a month from now by purchasing a CALL option for $.70 per share.

Options are sold in contracts of 100 shares per contract. Therefore, you could purchase the right to buy 200 shares of GE by purchasing 2 option contracts at $.70 per share. It is VERY important that you remember to only purchase 2 option contracts, not 200. Those 2 option contracts will cost you (200 * $.70) $140.00. So you now control $7,300.00 worth of GE stock for $140.00.

Since GE is trading right at the contract strike price (36.50) if you hold the option until expiration the stock would have to be trading at $37.20 for you to break even. Why? Because in order to take ownership of the stock you would have to pay $36.50 per share which is $36.50 * 200 which equals $7,300.00.

In addition remember you paid $140.00 for the option so your total expenditure is $7,300.00 plus $140.00 or $7,440.00. You can divide that by the number of shares (200) to get a break even price of $37.20. The most you can lose on this trade is the price of the calls you purchase or $140.00 using options. If you purchased the stock you could lose $7,300.00 if it went to $0.00.

Stock Price:	$36.50	200 Shares	$7,300.00
Option Price:	$ .70	200 Shares	$ 140.00
Break Even:	$37.20	200 Shares	$7,440.00

As you may have noticed you could have also just added the strike price of the option $36.50 to the price of the option $.70 to get the break even point. I was not trying to make it more difficult just to make sure you understood the math behind it.

A PUT option works in a similar fashion but it gives you the right to sell a stock at a given price instead of purchase it. A simple examine using GE from above let's assume you think the price is going down instead of up.

If you wanted to short (selling stock you don't own) you would probably need $7,300.00 in your account to cover the short position assuming your broker allowed you to short stocks. The other way to do this would be to purchase a PUT option at a strike of $36.50 for about $.65 with an expiration one month away.

You end up with the same position as if you shorted the stock but instead of risking $7,300.00 ($36.50 stock price* 200 shares) you are only risking $130.00 ($.65 option price * 200 shares). Please remember to purchase 2 contracts, not 200. In order for you to break even at expiration in a month the stock out have to be trading at $35.85 ($36.50 strike - $.65 option price). I just used the simple calculation this time for you.

It is important to understand the long calculation I used earlier so you can take into effect commissions.

You can also sell CALLS and PUTS which I will discuss later but those have increased risk.

You can buy and sell Calls and puts 'in the money', 'out of the money' or 'at the money'. When we purchased our GE Calls or Puts at a $36.50 strike with the underlying stock trading exactly at $36.50 that was 'at the money'. What that means is we were paying for time value only. With 'at the money' and 'out of the money' options you are just purchasing (or selling) time value.

If we had purchased our $36.50 Call when the stock was trading at $37.00 then $.50 ($37.00 -$36.50) would be the amount the option was 'in the money'. $.50 would be our intrinsic value and the rest of the option price would represent time value.

You can find a lot more information online about what options are and how they are priced. I will get into some of that later but this is not a book on option pricing models. If you really want to get into that there are many good reference tools out there.

As you may have guessed, I primarily trade options. But I do it in a wide variety of ways. In this book I am going to discuss my favorites and how I use them. Two of my favorite trading strategies are a variation of covered calls, butterflys and condors. Of course, this book is not about covered calls or any variation of them since we are going to focus on my range bound strategies.

One other thing I would like to point out is there are two types of options now available for trading. Weekly options which as the name implies expire weekly, every Friday.

The other type of option is a Monthly option which expires the third Friday of each month. I prefer to trade weekly options when I can because I like the shorter term. However, certain of my strategies require monthly options like condors and selling naked puts. As you learn my systems you can decide which you are more comfortable with and tailor your trading to how much trading you want to do. One big disadvantage to trading more often is the increased commissions you have to pay.

Chapter 2

Iron Condors - Indexes

Iron condors are a favorite of mine. I started out trading them on Indexes, made a lot of money and got cocky. Then, the market crashed and I was over extended trading SPX, RUT and NDX at the same time. I did not really have any rules and was trading them all wrong because some trading guru told me how to get into one. Didn't bother to tell me how to manage them.

I typically trade one strategy on indexes such as RUT, SPX and NDX and another on other types of stocks. I will describe my index Iron Condor strategy first.

First of all, I prefer SPX because I have found it trades more predictable to me. I seem to run into problems more often with RUT and NDX. That is not to say I do not trade them, just that I prefer the SPX.

An iron condor is a range bound strategy consisting short calls and puts and long calls and puts. Your outlook with a iron condor is direction neutral. You enter into an iron condor with a net credit. You need the security you are trading to stay within your short calls and puts. The long calls and puts are just to reduce your risk and margin requirements, otherwise it would be a strangle.

An iron condor has an identifiable maximum profit and maximum risk when you enter the trade, that is another good thing about them. I really do not mind having a capped profit potential if the returns are where I need them. The main thing I always try to get is a capped risk.

One strategy with an iron condor is to wait for expiration and keep all your initial credit. I rarely do that, I like to decide what return I need and put in a GTC order. When it hits, I get out.

About half the time I start an iron condor as an iron condor, the rest of the time I start with at put or call credit spread and then attempt to complete the other side to end up with my condor. If I do not get the fill I want on the second part of the condor, not a problem I just trade my credit spread.

I love trading condors on the major indexes because I have found them to be consistently profitable. At the time of writing this book my Iron Condors have been profitable 82.50% of the time over the past 40 trades. My annualized return for those trades has been 45.89% of my risk.

It is important to remember that is the return of my risk, not my entire account. I never trade all (or even an a large portion) of my account in one trade and neither should you.

My average risk over those trades was about $12,000.00 per trade. My average time in a condor is about 34 days.

My Profit/Loss ratio was about .58 which is not very good. But I want to be completely honest so I am sharing it with you. The reason for that is because I did not follow my own rules (see below) on some of my trades. If I had, my Profit/Loss ratio would have been MUCH better. This is important because I want you to remember, "Have a plan and stick to your plan!"

I do have some rules I try and follow when setting up an iron condor.

1. I like the delta of my short position to be 10 or less.
2. It is better to start your condor when volatility is high. You will actually make money as the volatility goes down.
3. Need at least 49 days until expiration but prefer not more than about 62.
4. It is better if you can see clear support and/or resistance on the chart protecting your positions.

When to adjust.

1. I typically try to adjust if the delta of one of my short positions goes above 30.
2. If the price gets too close to my short options. I cannot give you exactly what that number is because it is different depending on the security and volatility.

The second type of Iron Condor strategy that I use I primarily use on stocks and EFT's. We will get to that in the next section.

Ok, let's get started with some actual trade examples of how I trade Index Based Iron Condors.

The older trades show the actual contracts we traded. The newer ones I defaulted to 1 or 2 contracts because I wanted to make you focus more on the actual trade not the net profit. It is the percentages we want to focus on.

In my first Watch me Trade book, which the older trades are out of I used actual contracts, in my Watch me Trade 2 I shifted to a default number of contracts for the reason above regardless of how many I really traded in my account.

RUT 6/10/2016

On 6/10 the market had made a pretty good move down after an uptrend. I still believed that the market was in an uptrend and wanted to take advantage of the pull back to 'leg' into an Iron Condor. Legging in means that you place one side of the trade without initially placing the other side of the trade. It is not uncommon for me to enter a condor this way.

On 6/10 I placed an order to sell 10 contracts of the AUG16 $1020 Put and purchase the AUG16 $1000 Put to cover them with the RUT trading at $1162.91. I was able to bring in a credit of $1.50 per contract or $1,469.54 after commissions. My initial profit was my credit of $1,469.54 and my risk was $18,530.46 which would go down if I was able to sell a Call position later. Because $18,530.46 is my maximum risk during the trade that is the one I use to calculate my return.

On 6/20 I was able to get a $1.50 credit by selling the AUG16 $1250 Call and purchasing the AUG16 $1270 Call to cover it while the RUT was trading at $1167. This brought in another $1.50 per contract raising my potential profit to $2,939.08 after commissions. If I held to expiration I would have a 15.86%, although I had no intention of doing that. After my Calls filled I placed a GTC order to close at a debit of $1.45.

On 6/27 after the Britain EURO exit vote the RUT had dropped to $1096 getting close to a point when I would have to adjust the trade. I felt confident that market would rebound since nothing had fundamentally changed just because of the vote to exit. The market was panicking for no real reason. Fortunately, I was correct, on 6/29 the market was spiking up for the third straight day.

The market moved up to a range bound area after that. On 8/2 about three weeks before expiration my GTC order for $1.45 hit. After I bought back the position I was left with a profit of $1,428.13 after commissions. My return on risk was 7.71% for 53 days. Annualized that was about a 53.08% return.

Date		Exp.	Stk	$	CT		Cost	Balance
06/10/16	BO	AUG16	1000	-$6.80	10	Put	-$6,815.23	-$6,815.23
06/10/16	SO	AUG16	1020	$8.30	10	Put	$8,284.77	$1,469.54
06/20/16	BO	AUG16	1270	$1.50	10	Call	-$1,515.23	-$45.69
06/20/16	SO	AUG16	1250	$3.00	10	Call	$2,984.77	$2,939.08
08/02/16	BC	AUG16	1250	-$1.85	10	Call	-$1,865.23	$1,073.85
08/02/16	SC	AUG16	1270	$0.60	10	Call	$584.75	$1,658.60

08/02/16	BC	AUG16	1020	-$0.35	10	Put	-$365.23	$1,293.37
08/02/16	SC	AUG16	1000	$0.15	10	Put	$134.76	$1,428.13
							Profit:	$1,428.13

NDX – 6/17/2016

On 6/17 I decided to place an Iron Condor on NDX while it was trading at $4,371.20. Little did I know at the time this would become a nightmare trade for me. Most of the time when you have to defend an Iron Condor it is on the Put side which is usually easier to do because you can normally get better premiums on Puts and ranges further away. When you have to defend the Call side you do not get that luxury. That is normally not to bad, you just roll the Call to another month but on this trade NDX kept surging up with the rest of the market and left me scrambling for ways to keep this position profitable without increasing risk too much. I was lucky because I started this trade with only 1 contract because I had other positions open and I knew the Britain Euro vote was coming up. If I had started with more contracts I might have either had to close this at a loss at some point or sell off other positions to clear up margin. This is also the first time I ever had to defend my Calls multiple times in an Iron Condor.

You will notice in this trade that I increased contacts, rolled my Puts to bring in premium to offset losses on the Call side, increased the range on my Puts at one point instead of increasing the number of contracts and rolled to other months. In short, I did about everything you can do except close for a loss in my defense of this iron condor which makes it a good one to study.

This trade started on 6/17 with me placing a complete Iron Condor order using the AUG16 4700 and 4725 Calls and the 3800/3775 Puts. I put in an order for a $4.50 credit which was filled. That brought in a credit of $437.97 on an initial risk of $2,062.03 ($2500 - $437.97) which would have been a return of 21%. That was my initial mistake on this trade. I did not follow my own Iron Condor trading rules. I should have extended my range and shot for closer to a $3.00 credit. Even I still get greedy.

By 7/20 I was in trouble. Actually the warning signs started before then but I was hoping the market would move down since I only had about 30 days left on the AUG Calls. On 7/20 I made my first defensive move and rolled my 4700/4725 Calls up to 4775/4800 by doubling my Calls from one to two in order to stay in August. Nine days later on 7/29 the market had shot up again and I was forced to roll my 4775/4800 Calls to 4800/4825 by doubling them again to four contracts. Now my risk was about $9,600.00.

On 7/29 I also decided to roll my Puts up from 3800/3775 to 4475/4425 in order to bring in some additional premium. I also increased my range from 25 to 50 on these. I doubted the market would be going down and decided to increase the range instead of number of contracts. I also sold a second 4475/4425 Put on a separate trade after I rolled my first Put contracts. This gave me four outstanding Call contracts at a 25 range and two outstanding Put contracts at a 50 range.

On 8/5 my Calls were in trouble again and I did not want to increase risk anymore. Even if I had wanted to because of how little time was left on the AUG16 options it would have been hard to do. I decided to go ahead and roll my four 4825/4900 AUG16 calls to 4900/4925 SEP16 Calls. I was able to roll them up without increasing risk more by selling time. On 8/24 my 4475/4425 Puts expired worthless for I sold 4575/4550 SEP16 Puts to bring in some more premium.

On 9/8 I was finally able to exit this trade by closing all my position. At the end of August I had the potential to make $711.73 even after all my moves, but when I have to adjust I want out! I was able to give up about half of that to close the trade early and still keep $318.05 for a 3.419% return on 83 days. In truth I would have been ecstatic to have walked away at $0.00 by the end of July so making a little bit was a blessing.

Even if I had traded this correctly when I entered the trade I still would have had to adjust on this one. Sudden major market moves can really cause problems in Iron Condors. Especially if they are up moves when it comes to adjustment premium. The only good thing about an up move is you can typically wait a little longer for a pull back. In a market crash you sometimes wonder if it will ever end.

Date		Exp	Strike	Price	CT	C/P	Total	Balance
06/17/16	SO	AUG16	4700	$10.95	1	C	$1,091.98	$1,091.98
06/17/16	BO	AUG16	4725	-$8.15	1	C	-$818.01	$273.97
06/17/16	SO	AUG16	3800	$25.70	1	P	$2,566.99	$2,840.96
06/17/16	BO	AUG16	3775	-$24.00	1	P	-$2,402.99	$437.97
07/20/16	BC	AUG16	4700	-$42.52	1	C	-$4,254.27	-$3,816.30
07/20/16	SC	AUG16	4725	$32.04	1	C	$3,201.74	-$614.56
07/20/16	SO	AUG16	4775	$17.05	2	C	$3,405.47	$2,790.91
07/20/16	BO	AUG16	4800	-$12.15	2	C	-$2,434.53	$356.38
07/29/16	BC	AUG16	4775	-$28.24	2	C	-$5,651.05	-$5,294.67
07/29/16	SC	AUG16	4800	$18.96	2	C	$3,788.96	-$1,505.71
07/29/16	SO	AUG16	4825	$12.54	4	C	$5,009.93	$3,504.22
07/29/16	BO	AUG16	4850	-$7.90	4	C	-$3,166.07	$338.15
07/29/16	BO	AUG16	4425	-$5.60	1	P	-$565.25	-$227.10
07/29/16	SO	AUG16	4475	$7.56	1	P	$750.76	$523.66
07/29/16	BC	AUG16	3800	-$0.59	1	P	-$62.02	$461.64
07/29/16	SC	AUG16	3775	$0.54	1	P	$50.99	$512.63

07/29/16	SO	AUG16	4475	$7.52	1	P	$748.99	$1,261.62
07/29/16	BO	AUG16	4425	-$5.62	1	P	-$564.99	$696.63
08/05/16	BC	AUG16	4825	-$18.85	4	C	-$7,545.34	-$6,848.71
08/05/16	SC	AUG16	4850	$11.10	4	C	$4,434.67	-$2,414.04
08/05/16	SO	SEP16	4900	$26.03	4	C	$10,406.67	$7,992.63
08/05/16	BO	SEP16	4925	-$19.28	4	C	-$7,717.31	$275.32
08/24/16	BO	SEP16	4550	-$9.90	3	P	-$2,976.80	-$2,701.48
08/24/16	SO	SEP16	4575	$11.40	3	P	$3,413.21	$711.73
09/08/16	BC	SEP16	4900	-$1.08	1	C	-$113.25	$598.48
09/08/16	SC	SEP16	4925	$0.43	1	C	$37.76	$636.24
09/08/16	BC	SEP16	4900	-$1.07	3	C	-$327.56	$308.68
09/08/16	SC	SEP16	4925	$0.40	3	C	$119.45	$423.13
09/08/16	SC	SEP16	4550	$1.63	3	P	$480.45	$908.58
09/08/16	BC	SEP16	4575	-$1.96	3	P	-$590.53	$318.05
						Profit:	$318.05	

SPX – 6/23/16

I placed this Iron Condor the day before the Britain European Union exit vote. This could have been considered a high risk trade, except I legged into it. I sold my Calls on 6/23 and waited until 6/24 to sell my Puts. I was able to take advantage of the market panic sell, since I believed it would bounce back up quickly I was happy to do so. In the end this was one of my best Condor trades. Things worked out better than I could have hoped as you will see.

SPX was trading at $2,104.48 on 6/23/16. I sold 10 August 2016 expiration $2215 Calls and purchased the $2240 Calls to cover them for about $1.80 per contract. My risk was $23,304.90 with a potential profit of $1,695.10 on just my calls. On 6/24 the SPX had dropped to $2,051.00 and volatility was moving up because of the drop. Because of the volatility being so high I was able to sell the August 2016 $1760 Puts and buy the August 2016 $1735 Puts to cover them for about $1.00 in more premium. The high volatility allowed me to pick a strike $291.00 away from where the SPX was currently trading and bring in another $1,395.10 in premium making my potential profit $3,090.20 and reducing my risk to $21,909.80. If I held until expiration my return would be about 14%.

After I my Puts filled I placed a GTC order to close this position at a debit of $1.25. On 6/28 with the market rebounding nicely my GTC order filled and I pocketed $1,719.90 in just 5 days. A return of about 7.5% on my initial risk of $23,304.90. They do not all work out this way, but when they do it is great.

Date		Exp	Strike	Price	CT	Type	Cost	Balance
06/23/16	BO	AUG16	2240	-$2.00	10	Call	-$2,052.50	-$2,052.50
06/23/16	SO	AUG16	2215	$3.80	10	Call	$3,747.60	$1,695.10
06/24/16	BO	AUG16	1735	-$10.00	10	Put	-$10,052.50	-$8,357.40
06/24/16	SO	AUG16	1760	$11.00	10	Put	$11,447.60	$3,090.20
06/28/16	BC	AUG16	2215	-$0.55	10	Call	-$580.02	$2,510.18
06/28/16	BC	AUG16	1760	-$6.25	10	Put	-$6,280.10	-$3,769.92
06/28/16	SC	AUG16	1735	$5.20	10	Put	$5,169.90	$1,399.98
06/28/16	S	AUG16	2240	$0.35	10	Call	$320.10	$1,720.08

	C						
						Profit:	$1,720.08

SPY – 07/19/2016

This is another trade you should not attempt. I traded this one in my virtual account to show how difficult it is to make a decent return with an EFT. I normally only do Iron Condors on indexes. The other thing I did here was a short term two week expiration which I do not recommend for Iron Condors. There are people that trade weekly or shorter term Iron Condors and make money, but I find it too difficult and you have to watch them constantly. Not the way I like to trade Iron Condors, if I have to defend one I am in a bad position already. With short term ones you will defend far to many.

With SPY trading at $215.80 I placed my Iron Condor by selling the 216.50 Call and covering it with the 217 Call. I also sold the 216 Put and purchased the 215.50 Put to cover it. Not a normally Iron condor set up with SPY at $215.80 but I thought it was going up.

In the end I did make money but it was more due to a drop in volatility than anything else. I sold the position at the best possible time and got lucky 14 days later. I made $310.00 not including commissions. If I traded this in my cheapest commission account I would have probable netted $260.00 because of the number of contracts. Still not a bad return but I have not found short term condors worth my time and effort as a whole.

Date		Exp	Strike	Price	CT	Type	Cost	Balance
07/16/16	BO	8WK1	217	-$1.28	10	Call	-$1,280.00	-$1,280.00
07/16/16	SO	8WK1	216.5	$1.53	10	Call	$1,530.00	$250.00
07/16/16	SO	8WK1	216	$2.02	10	Put	$2,020.00	$2,270.00
07/16/16	BO	8WK1	215.5	-$1.82	10	Put	-$1,820.00	$450.00
08/02/16	SC	8WK1	217	$0.45	10	Call	$450.00	$900.00

08/02/16	BC	8WK1	216.5	-$0.55	10	Call	-$550.00	$350.00
08/02/16	BC	8WK1	216	-$1.40	10	Put	-$1,140.00	-$790.00
08/02/16	SC	8WK1	215.5	$1.10	10	Put	$1,100.00	$310.00
							Profit:	$310.00

SPX – 4/24/17

Saw an opportunity on the Put side for a possible condor. I was able to get my Puts filled on 4/24, so I entered an order in on the Call side. I was fine with just a Put spread if I could not get a Condor going. This is a common way I enter into a condor instead of placing an actual condor order.

I like to wait for a sharp move down to fill my Puts as low as possible then try to get the call side if I can get the premium I want.

When I entered the trade I had a potential profit of $350.00 if I held until expiration. However I normally place a GTC close order after I enter a condor and wait for it to be filled. On 5/9/17, just 15 days later, I hit my profit target of $180.00. My risk on this one was $2,150.00 which gave me a return of 8.37% over that 15 day period.

Date		Exp.	Strike	Price	CT	Type	Cost	Balance
04/24/17	BO	JUN17	2125	-$4.50	1	Put	-$450.00	-$450.00
04/24/17	SO	JUN17	2150	$6.50	1	Put	$650.00	$200.00
04/25/17	SO	JUN17	2475	$3.70	1	Call	$370.00	$570.00
04/25/17	B	JUN17	2500	-$2.20	1	Call	-$220.00	$350.00

	O							
05/09/17	BC	JUN17	2150	-$2.15	1	Put	-$215.00	$135.00
05/09/17	SC	JUN17	2125	$1.65	1	Put	$165.00	$300.00
05/09/17	SC	JUN17	2500	$1.05	1	Call	$105.00	$405.00
05/09/17	BC	JUN17	2475	-$2.25	1	Call	-$215.00	$180.00
							Profit:	$180.00

SPX – 07/31/2018 – Iron Condor

I started this trade looking for an Iron Condor, I entered the Put side first and was filled in about a day. Next I entered an order for my Calls but … I was never able to get filled at a level I was comfortable with.

SPX was trading near all time highs and I just could not get the Call side I wanted. Therefore, this trade ended up being a Bull Put Credit Spread. I decided to leave it in the Condor section because it was meant as an Condor.

When I entered my Puts, SPX was trading at $2816.00. I sold the 9/21/18 $2620/$2595 spread for $1.25. My total risk was $11,906.25 with a credit of $593.75.

If I held to close my return would be about 4.9%. I set a GTC order to keep a 3.67% return and waited.

On 8/15 SPX had a fairly large down day. It hit $2800 but was still a LONG way away from threatening my short Put.

On 8/27 SPX spiked up to $2895 and my GTC order hit, closing me out for my target profit.

Date		EXP	Strike	Price	Ct	C/P	Cost	Balance
07/31/18	SO	09/21/18	2620	10.4	5	P	$5,196.75	$5,196.75
07/31/18	BO	09/21/18	2595	9.15	5	P	-$4,603.00	$593.75
08/27/18	BC	09/21/18	2620	2.1	5	P	-$1,053.25	-$459.50
08/27/18	SC	09/21/18	2595	1.85	5	P	$897.00	$437.50
							Profit of	$437.50

SPX – 08/28/18 – Iron Condor

Once the above trade closed I immediately started looking for my next Condor in SPX. Once again I started with one side of the trade only. This time because SPX was spiking up I was able to get into the Call side of the trade first.

On 8/28 with SPX at $2900.35 I got my Call spread of $3030/$3040 filled for $.60.

It took me two days to get into the Put side of the trade. I had to adjust my strikes up a few times and lower my credit but I finally got the trade filled. Did not get the fills I wanted but I still feel pretty good about the position.

On 8/30 with SPX at $2901.50 I got my Put spread of $2705/$2695 filled for $.50.

If I held to close that would be about a 11.7% return on my risk. However, I set a GTC Order to keep about one half of my initial credit.

In the end my GTC hit on 9/17 and I ended this trade with a profit of $203.95 or 5.7% on a trade that lasted 20 days. This was a pretty simple SPX Iron Condor, I wish they all ended this way.

Date		EXP	Strike	Price	Ct	C/P	Cost	Balance
08/28/18	BO	10/19/18	3040	$3.48	4	C	-$1,394.65	-$1,394.65
08/28/18	SO	10/19/18	3030	$4.08	4	C	$1,624.40	$229.75
08/30/18	SO	10/19/18	2705	$10.00	4	P	$3,997.35	$4,227.10
08/30/18	BO	10/19/18	2695	$9.50	4	P	-$3,807.60	$419.50
09/17/18	SC	10/19/18	3040	$1.55	4	C	$617.35	$1,036.85
09/17/18	BC	10/19/18	3030	$1.80	4	C	-$722.65	$314.20
09/17/18	BC	10/19/18	2705	$4.70	4	P	-$1,882.65	-$1,568.45
09/17/18	SC	10/19/18	2695	$4.45	4	P	$1,772.40	$203.95
						Profit of:	$203.95

SPX – 9/17/18 – Iron Condor

This was one of my most difficult trades of the year. It was an SPX Iron Condor which I have pretty strict rules for trading but it was moving up and then down so fast that I struggled to trade my rules.

On 9/17 with SPX trading at $2902.00 I entered an Iron Condor expecting easy profits like I had seen throughout the year trading these. I started the trade by selling the $3020.00 Call and buying the $3035.00 Call to cover while selling the $2675.00 Put and buy the $2660.00 Put to cover it.

On 9/20 SPX spiked up to $2932.00 putting my short Call delta at 20, I try to adjust around 30.

On 10/3 SPX was up to $2937.39 but my short Call delta had dropped a little to 18 as the market was slowing down and time had passed. I love time decay on these.

By 10/11 SPX had dropped from $2937.39 to $2771.00, my Calls were fine now but my short Put was in trouble with a delta of 28 which increased to 31 during that day. Time to look for an adjustment.

On 10/12 I was able to roll my Puts from from 11/16 to 12/7 and from 2675/2660 to 2650/2630. I increased the spread from 15 to 20 which increased my risk for a net credit which was nice, except for the increased risk! But at least I managed to move the short Put down from 2675 to 2650.

On 10/23 SPX moved against me again down to $2700.00. I rolled my Calls down 100 points and increased their spread from 15 to 20 to match my calls to bring in a credit in order to adjust my Puts again!

I then rolled my Puts down another 50 points from 2650/2630 to 2600/2580 and my expiration from 12/7 to 12/14. I was still able to bring in a net credit from my 10/23 rolls.

On 10/25 SPX spiked down yet again to $2648.00, my short Put delta spiked up to 33 (over my 30 adjustment level). However, because I had moved down twice already I really felt the market might cooperate and move up for me. By the end of the day the market had bounced up to $2686.00 and my short Put delta was now right at 30.0

On 10/26 SPX moved down to $2640.00 and I decided to move the Puts down again and from 12/14 to 12/21 from 2600/2580 to 2570/2550. Surely this would be enough! I kept my Calls where they were because I still had a credit on this trade and was afraid it would make a rapid move up.

On 11/8 SPX spiked up to $2811.00 now and my Calls were moving toward a 30 delta on my short Call.

On 11/18 SPX had begun to pull back. I decided to roll my Call out so they would be on the same expiration as my Puts (makes closing easier) but did not roll them up. I rolled my Calls from 12/14 to 12/21 expiration.

On 11/20 SPX had dropped big over the past couple of days and my short Put delta was at 33. I decided to wait and see because of how much I had moved down already. I really felt the market was WAY oversold and there just could not be that much downward pressure left.

On 11/26 my GTC order FINALLY hit and I closed at about break even. Remember, once I make a single adjustment I move my GTC to break even to just get out of the trade as soon as possible.

I ended up with a $24.00 profit on a risk of $5001.00 or about 0.48% over 70 days. Of course, the profit here is not what is important. What is important is that I kept from losing money and came very close to following my trading rules.

When my trade finally closed SPX was at $2673.00.

Date		EXP	Strike	Price	Ct	C/P	Cost	Balance
09/17/18	SO	11/16/18	$3,020.00	$5.24	3	C	$1,572.00	$1,572.00
09/17/18	BO	11/16/18	$3,035.00	$3.97	3	C	-$1,191.00	$381.00
09/17/18	SO	11/16/18	$2,675.00	$10.74	3	P	$3,222.00	$3,603.00
09/17/18	BO	11/16/18	$2,660.00	$9.96	3	P	-$3,000.00	$603.00
10/12/18	BC	11/16/18	$2,675.00	$34.96	3	P	-$10,494.00	-$9,891.00
10/12/18	SC	11/16/18	$2,660.00	$31.69	3	P	$9,507.00	-$384.00
10/12/18	SO	12/07/18	$2,650.00	$39.99	3	P	$11,997.00	$11,613.00
10/12/18	BO	12/07/18	$2,630.00	$36.07	3	P	-$10,827.00	$786.00
10/12/18	BC	11/16/18	$3,020.00	$0.80	3	C	-$246.00	$540.00
10/12/18	SC	11/16/18	$3,035.00	$0.65	3	C	$195.00	$735.00
10/12/18	SO	12/07/18	$2,980.00	$3.50	3	C	$1,050.00	$1,785.00
10/12/18	BO	12/07/18	$3,000.00	$2.60	3	C	-$786.00	$999.00

10/23/18	BC	12/07/18	$2,980.00	$1.03	3	C	-$315.00	$684.00
10/23/18	SC	12/07/18	$3,000.00	$0.73	3	C	$219.00	$903.00
10/23/18	SO	12/14/18	$2,880.00	$7.20	3	C	$2,160.00	$3,063.00
10/23/18	BO	12/14/18	$2,900.00	$5.20	3	C	-$1,566.00	$1,497.00
10/23/18	BC	12/07/18	$2,650.00	$56.27	3	P	-$16,887.00	-$15,390.00
10/23/18	SC	12/07/18	$2,630.00	$50.54	3	P	$15,162.00	-$228.00
10/23/18	SO	12/14/18	$2,600.00	$47.29	3	P	$14,187.00	$13,959.00
10/23/18	BO	12/14/18	$2,580.00	$42.86	3	P	-$12,864.00	$1,095.00
10/26/18	BC	12/14/18	$2,600.00	$55.65	3	P	-$16,701.00	-$15,606.00
10/26/18	SC	12/14/18	$2,580.00	$50.05	3	P	$15,015.00	-$591.00
10/26/18	SO	12/21/18	$2,570.00	$52.05	3	P	$15,615.00	$15,024.00
10/26/18	BO	12/21/18	$2,550.00	$47.20	3	P	-$14,166.00	$858.00
11/18/18	BC	12/14/18	$2,880.00	$16.26	3	C	-$4,878.00	-$4,020.00
11/18/18	SC	12/14/18	$2,900.00	$10.89	3	C	$3,267.00	-$753.00
11/18/18	SO	12/21/18	$2,880.00	$21.19	3	C	$6,537.00	$5,604.00
11/18/18	BO	12/21/18	$2,900.00	$15.02	3	C	-$4,518.00	$1,086.00
11/26/18	BC	12/21/18	$2,880.00	$1.10	3	C	-$330.00	$756.00
11/26/18	SC	12/21/18	$2,900.00	$0.75	3	C	$225.00	$981.00
11/26/18	BC	12/21/18	$2,570.00	$17.85	3	P	-$5,355.00	-$4,374.00
11/26/18	SC	12/21/18	$2,550.00	$14.70	3	P	$4,422.00	$24.00

						Profit of:	$24.00

SPX – 11/27/18 – Iron Condor

This is one of my monthly SPX Iron Condor trades and for the second month in a row I struggled with it. Normally about one or maybe two a year give me a problem, kind of rare to have two in a row but that is the way the market moves sometimes.

Because I had such difficulty with the last SPX Iron Condor I was expecting an easy time with this one on 11/27 when I placed the trade. With SPX at $2682.20 and Implied Volatility at 28 I sold the 1/18/19 $2870 Call and purchased the $2890 Call. I sold the $2400 Put and bought the $2380 Put. Both of my shorts were at around Delta 10 to 12 which was just what the strategy called for.

My initial credit was $602.00 on a risk of $3398.00, I set a GTC to keep about half of it. When I entered this trade it showed a 74.39% probability of success if held to expiration.

At one time this trade was showing a $200.00 profit but by 12/20 that had changed. With SPX down at 2470 my short Put Delta was at 32 so I started looking for an adjustment. I rolled my Puts down and out a week from 1/18 to 1/25 and down from 2400/2380 to 2360/2340 for about a $1.00 debit. I left my calls for the time being hoping for move back up so I could roll them down to get them on the same cycle.

On 12/27 SPX spiked up 100 points and I rolled my Calls to the 1/25 expiration and down from 2870/2890 to 2720/2740 for a $.65 credit.

This move reduced my potential profit but that did not really matter that much since my rules say if I have to adjust I change my GTC to about break even, which I did.

On 01/04/19 my GTC order hit and I closed this trade for a $28.00 profit or 0.82% over 38 days. Not much of a profit but no losses and I defended this trade successfully.

Date		EXP	Strike	Price	Ct	C/P	Cost	Balance
11/27/18	SO	01/18/19	$2,870.00	$6.05	2	C	$1,210.00	$1,210.00
11/27/18	BO	01/18/19	$2,890.00	$4.30	2	C	-$868.00	$342.00
11/27/18	SO	01/18/19	$2,400.00	$11.35	2	P	$2,270.00	$2,612.00
11/27/18	BO	01/18/19	$2,380.00	$10.05	2	P	-$2,010.00	$602.00
12/20/18	BC	01/18/19	$2,400.00	$37.25	2	P	-$7,452.00	-$6,850.00
12/20/18	SC	01/18/19	$2,380.00	$32.40	2	P	$6,480.00	-$370.00
12/20/18	SO	01/25/19	$2,360.00	$33.10	2	P	$6,620.00	$6,250.00
12/20/18	BO	01/25/19	$2,340.00	$29.25	2	P	-$5,852.00	$398.00
12/27/18	BC	01/18/19	$2,870.00	$0.30	2	C	-$60.00	$338.00
12/27/18	SC	01/18/19	$2,890.00	$0.15	2	C	$30.00	$368.00
12/27/18	SO	01/25/19	$2,720.00	$3.05	2	C	$610.00	$978.00
12/27/18	BO	01/25/19	$2,740.00	$2.25	2	C	-$458.00	$520.00
01/04/19	BC	01/25/19	$2,720.00	$0.55	2	C	-$110.00	$410.00
01/04/19	SC	01/25/19	$2,740.00	$0.40	2	C	$80.00	$490.00
01/04/19	BC	01/25/19	$2,360.00	$13.05	2	P	-$2,610.00	-$2,120.00
01/04/19	SC	01/25/19	$2,340.00	$10.75	2	P	$2,148.00	$28.00
							Profit of:	$28.00

Chapter 3

Iron Condors – Non-Index

My non-index Iron Condors are based on a probability strategy. I use the TDAmeritrade platform to determine the probability that a security will finish within a given price range at expiration.

Some basic rules.

1. Use stocks with highly liquid options. You need this to get good fills when you open and close.

2. Try to get a probability of at least 65% when you open the trade. Right now my average beginning trade probability is about 67.15%.

3. Try to get at least a 25% credit based on risk. If you are risking $500.00 you want a credit of about $125.00 to enter the trade. Right now we are at about 38.68% when we enter the trade.

4. Set a Good to Cancel (GTC) order for about half of your initial credit as soon as you enter the trade. Our potential return when we start the trade is 38.68%, our actual return based on our GTC order is 16.58%. Not quite half, so you see sometimes we adjust depending on the market. These types of adjustments are more a gut feel than anything else. You will learn them over time.

5. Try to use stocks that are in top third of their implied volatility. At least top half. This is not a hard and fast rule but it really helps.

6. Don't over trade. We typically don't adjust these trades so you either win or lose. We try to keep our risk to about 1% of our portfolio, maybe 2% at the most.

When to Adjust.

1. We typically don't. You either win or lose.

2. Sometimes if we can roll for a credit we might roll out a losing trade the final week. If we cannot roll for a credit we close and take the loss.

When to Close.

1. When you GTC order is hit.

2. The day of expiration if you don't roll. Close and take your loss or whatever small gain you have. In fact, you could close anytime the week of expiration if you are showing a gain and are worried the security might move to a loss.

The older trades show the actual contracts we traded. The newer ones I defaulted to 1 or 2 contracts because I wanted to make you focus more on the actual trade not the net profit. It is the percentages we want to focus on.

In my first Watch me Trade book, which the older trades are out of I used actual contracts, in my Watch me Trade 2 I shifted to a default number of contracts for the reason above regardless of how many I really traded in my account.

GLD – 8/25/16

Decided to enter a GLD Iron Condor. I normally do not like trading condor's on anything but the indexes and maybe SPY, DIA or QQQ. However I decided to try my hand at a GLD trade. Overall the trade was successful with a respectable return for a 30 day trade, but I am still not fond of trading condors outside my comfort zone unless everything lines up perfectly.

Most of the time when I enter a condor I set my close price. Usually 25% to 50% of the potential. When that hits I let it close automatically.

Overall risk was $4,000.00 minus the credit I received of $350.00 or $3,650.00. I closed with a profit of $270.00 or a return of 7.4% for a 28 day investment. About 96.43% annualized.

Date	Exp.		Strike	Price	CT	Type	Cost	Balance
08/25/16	BO	OCT16	112	-$.14	10	Put	-$140.00	-$140.00
08/25/16	SO	OCT16	116	$.34	10	Put	$340.00	$200.00
08/25/16	SO	OCT16	140	$.41	10	Call	$410.00	$610.00
08/25/16	BO	OCT16	144	-$.26	10	Call	-$260.00	$350.00
09/22/16	SC	OCT16	144	$.02	10	Call	$20.00	$370.00
09/22/16	BC	OCT16	140	-$.07	10	Call	-$70.00	$300.00
09/22/16	BC	OCT16	116	-$.04	10	Put	-$40.00	$260.00
09/22/16	SC	OCT16	112	$.01	10	Put	$10.00	$270.00
							Profit:	$270.00

EWZ – 9/4/18 – Iron Condor

Saw a quick opportunity to get into a high probability trade on EWZ. The implied volatility looked good and the chart supported my short positions.

On 9/4 I sold the 10/19 $37 Call and purchased the $40 Call to cover it. At the same time I sold the 10/19 $27 Put and purchased the $23 Put to finish up the condor with EWZ trading at $31.36. I had a pretty good profit zone and everything worked out great when the trade hit my GTC on 9/19, just 15 days later.

I finished with a profit of $44.00 on an initial risk of $311.00 or about 14% return. EWZ was trading at $32.73 when I closed.

Date		EXP	Strike	Price	Ct	C/P	Cost	Balance
09/04/18	SO	10/19/18	$37.00	$0.54	1	C	$54.00	$54.00
09/04/18	BO	10/19/18	$40.00	$0.21	1	C	-$21.00	$33.00
09/04/18	SO	10/19/18	$27.00	$0.74	1	P	$74.00	$107.00
09/04/18	BO	10/19/18	$23.00	$0.14	1	P	-$18.00	$89.00
09/19/18	BC	10/19/18	$37.00	$0.37	1	C	-$37.00	$52.00
09/19/18	SC	10/19/18	$40.00	$0.07	1	C	$7.00	$59.00
09/19/18	BC	10/19/18	$27.00	$0.18	1	P	-$18.00	$41.00
09/19/18	SC	10/19/18	$23.00	$0.03	1	P	$3.00	$44.00
							Profit of:	$44.00

DIA – 9/4/18 – Iron Condor

I started this trade with DIA trading at $259.18 and it did not go as smoothly as some of my others. On 10/3 I was considering rolling this trade out another month or closing for a small profit.

In the end I decided to hold and let the probabilities play out a little longer. DIA cooperated and pulled back and hit my updated GTC order on 10/8. I say updated because I decided to take less profit on the pull back as opposed to holding to see what happened. Perhaps I got a little lucky here or perhaps the percentages favored me.

I closed this trade for a $64.00 profit on a risk of $756.00 or 8.47% over 34 days.

Date		EXP	Strike	Price	Ct	C/P	Cost	Balance
09/04/18	BO	10/19/18	$244.00	$1.12	2	C	-$224.00	-$224.00
09/04/18	SO	10/19/18	$249.00	$1.62	2	C	$324.00	$100.00
09/04/18	SO	10/19/18	$267.00	$1.14	2	P	$228.00	$328.00
09/04/18	BO	10/19/18	$272.00	$0.42	2	P	-$84.00	$244.00
10/08/18	BC	10/19/18	$267.00	$0.85	2	C	-$170.00	$74.00
10/08/18	SC	10/19/18	$272.00	$0.15	2	C	$30.00	$104.00
10/08/18	BC	10/19/18	$249.00	$0.47	2	P	-$94.00	$10.00
10/08/18	SC	10/19/18	$244.00	$0.27	2	P	$54.00	$64.00
							Profit of:	$64.00

HD – 9/05/18 – Iron Condor

On 9/5 I decided to place an Iron Condor trade on HD. HD was trading at $204.27 with an implied volatility rank of 13, not great but I decided to go with it anyway.

When I placed the trade I had a 60.5% probability of success if I held to expiration.

I sold the 10/19 $215 Call and purchased the $220.00 Call to cover it, then sold the 10/19 $195 Put and purchased the $190 Put to finish up my Iron Condor.

On 9/25 my GTC order hit and I was able to close the trade for a profit after just 20 days. I made $39.00 on a risk of $385.00 or about 10.13%. The overall return was a little lower than I prefer but at least I made money.

Date		EXP	Strike	Price	Ct	C/P	Cost	Balance
09/05/18	SO	10/19/18	$215.00	$1.12	1	C	$112.00	$112.00
09/05/18	BO	10/19/18	$220.00	$0.53	1	C	-$53.00	$59.00
09/05/18	SO	10/19/18	$195.00	$1.50	1	P	$150.00	$209.00
09/05/18	BO	10/19/18	$190.00	$0.90	1	P	-$94.00	$115.00
09/25/18	BC	10/19/18	$215.00	$0.82	1	C	-$82.00	$33.00
09/25/18	SC	10/19/18	$220.00	$0.29	1	C	$29.00	$62.00
09/25/18	BC	10/19/18	$195.00	$0.43	1	P	-$47.00	$15.00
09/25/18	SC	10/19/18	$190.00	$0.24	1	P	$24.00	$39.00
							Profit of:	$39.00

QQQ – 9/10/18 – Iron Condor

Decided to place a QQQ trade on 9/10, really the credit I got was not all that great when I entered the trade. I was trying to stay in the market and liked the strikes I was able to get so decided to go for it.

When I entered this trade it had about a 66% chance of success if held to expiration. With QQQ trading at $181.35 I sold the 10/26 $192.50 Call and purchased the $195.00 Call to cover it. I finished out my Iron Condor by selling the $170.00 Put and purchasing the $167.50 Put.

Part of the reason my credit wasn't all that great was because I used a $2.50 spread. A larger spread would have given me a larger credit.

I was able to close this trade on 10/4 for a profit of $42.00 or about 10.50%.

Date	EXP	Strike	Price	Ct	C/P	Cost	Balance

09/10/18	SO	10/26/18	$192.50	$0.47	2	C	$94.00	$94.00
09/10/18	BO	10/26/18	$195.00	$0.33	2	C	-$46.00	$48.00
09/10/18	SO	10/26/18	$170.00	$1.55	2	P	$310.00	$358.00
09/10/18	BO	10/26/18	$167.50	$1.25	2	P	-$258.00	$100.00
10/04/18	BC	10/26/18	$192.50	$0.26	2	C	-$52.00	$48.00
10/04/18	SC	10/26/18	$195.00	$0.10	2	C	$20.00	$68.00
10/04/18	BC	10/26/18	$170.00	$0.38	2	P	-$76.00	-$8.00
10/04/18	SC	10/26/18	$167.50	$0.29	2	P	$50.00	$42.00
						Profit of:	$42.00

PBR – 09/20/18 – Iron Condor

On 9/20 we decided to place an Iron Condor in PBR with its Implied Volatility at 63.04. Our initial trade probability was 75.67% which was better than normal for these types of trades, so we figured what could go wrong?

With PBR at $11.29 we sold the 11/2/18 $13.50 Call and purchased the $14.50 Call. We then sold the $9.00 Put and purchased the $8.00 Put to enter the trade with a total credit of $.36. We did increased contracts because the spread was only $1.00. In retrospect this was not a good trade, so you won't see this one again.

On 10/24 PBR was trading at $15.60 and we were almost at max loss on this trade so we started seeing if we could find a roll for a credit. We got lucky and did.

We rolled out from 11/2/18 to 11/30/18 selling time. We were also able to roll up our calls from 13.50/14.50 to 14.00/15.00 increasing our chance of success.

On 11/30 (expiration day) we managed to close this trade with PBR trading at $14.27 for a small profit.

After 71 days we closed with a profit of $24.00 or 9.3% on our initial risk of $256.00

Date		EXP	Strike	Price	Ct	C/P	Cost	Balance
09/20/18	BO	11/02/18	$8.00	$0.14	4	P	-$56.00	-$56.00
09/20/18	SO	11/02/18	$9.00	$0.32	4	P	$128.00	$72.00
09/20/18	SO	11/02/18	$13.50	$0.45	4	C	$180.00	$252.00
09/20/18	BO	11/02/18	$14.50	$0.27	4	C	-$108.00	$144.00
10/24/18	BC	11/02/18	$13.50	$2.27	4	C	-$908.00	-$764.00
10/24/18	SC	11/02/18	$14.50	$1.42	4	C	$568.00	-$196.00
10/24/18	BC	11/02/18	$9.00	$0.01	4	P	-$4.00	-$200.00
10/24/18	SC	11/02/18	$8.00	$0.00	4	P	$0.00	-$200.00
10/24/18	SO	11/30/18	$14.00	$2.12	4	C	$848.00	$648.00
10/24/18	BO	11/30/18	$15.00	$1.44	4	C	-$576.00	$72.00
10/24/18	SO	11/30/18	$14.00	$0.45	4	P	$180.00	$252.00
10/24/18	BO	11/30/18	$13.00	$0.26	4	P	-$104.00	$148.00
11/30/18	BC	11/30/18	$14.00	$0.29	4	C	-$116.00	$32.00
11/30/18	SC	11/30/18	$15.00	$0.01	4	C	$4.00	$36.00
11/30/18	BC	11/30/18	$14.00	$0.04	4	P	-$16.00	$20.00
11/30/18	SC	11/30/18	$13.00	$0.01	4	P	$4.00	$24.00
							Profit of:	$24.00

CRM – 9/28/18 – Iron Condor

I have always struggling trading CRM, not sure why I keep trying. The return here looked pretty good, I guess that is one reason I keep trying to trade it.

On 9/28 I entered into a 11/16 Iron Condor selling the $175 Call and purchasing the $180 Call. I sold the $150 Put and purchased the $145 Put for a total of a $1.30 credit on a $3.70 risk per contract.

CRM had an implied volatility of 28.6 when I started the trade and a probability of success of 62.68%. My break even points were at $148.68 and $176.28. CRM was trading at $159.44 when I started the trade.

On 11/8 CRM was trading at $142.47 about half way between my short and long Puts. I decided to try and roll the position out to 12/21 if I could do it for a credit. I was lucky (or at least I thought I was) and was able to roll the entire position to 12/21 keeping the same strikes.

By 12/17 CRM was trading at $127.97, well below both my short and long Put, I had known for some time I had no hope of rolling the position so I was just waiting until 12/21 to close everything. Unfortunately someone decided to assign me my short Put and I ended up owning the shares. I promptly sold the shares and my remaining long Put to close that side of the trade. I just let the Calls expire worthless, the weren't worth the commissions to close.

I took a 100% loss of $370.00 on this trade that lasted 81 days.

Date		EXP	Strike	Price	Ct	C/P	Cost	Balance
09/28/18	SO	11/16/18	$175.00	$1.07	1	C	$107.00	$107.00
09/28/18	BO	11/16/18	$180.00	$0.60	1	C	-$62.00	$45.00
09/28/18	SO	11/16/18	$150.00	$2.18	1	P	$218.00	$263.00

Date	B/S	Exp	Strike	Price	Qty	P/C	Amount	Running
09/28/18	BO	11/16/18	$145.00	$1.35	1	P	-$137.00	$126.00
11/05/18	BC	11/16/18	$175.00	$0.03	1	C	-$3.00	$123.00
11/05/18	SC	11/16/18	$180.00	$0.02	1	C	$2.00	$125.00
11/05/18	SO	12/21/18	$165.00	$0.68	1	C	$68.00	$193.00
11/05/18	BO	12/21/18	$170.00	$0.39	1	C	-$43.00	$150.00
11/05/18	BC	12/21/18	$150.00	$7.80	1	P	-$780.00	-$630.00
11/05/18	SC	12/21/18	$145.00	$3.85	1	P	$385.00	-$245.00
11/05/18	SO	12/21/18	$155.00	$14.45	1	P	$1,445.00	$1,200.00
11/05/18	BO	12/21/18	$150.00	$10.65	1	P	-$1,069.00	$131.00
12/17/18		Put	Assigned		100		-$15,500.00	-$15,369.00
12/18/18	SC	STC		$18.65	1	P	$1,865.00	-$13,504.00
12/18/18	SE	Sell	Shares	$131.34	100		$13,134.00	-$370.00
						Loss of:	-$370.00

EWZ – 9/28/18 – Iron Condor

Looking to stay active I decided on an Iron Condor in EWZ on 9/28. Implied Volatility was at 79 and coming down from 100 so there was good premium still to be had.

With EWZ trading at $34.14 I sold the 11/16 $40 Call and purchased the $43 Call. I also sold the $29 Put and purchased the $26 Put to finish out my Iron Condor.

My break even was $28.06 and $40.94 which I felt pretty good about going into the trade. I set my GTC order at about 50% of my potential $180.00 maximum gain with a risk of $412.00.

EWZ had been down when I entered the trade and made a larger move to the upside than I felt it would. I had been in this trade a long time on 11/8 so I decided to get out of it instead of letting the odds play out for a small profit. Might have been alright to have stayed in but with expiration closing in and because of the length of the trade I decided to close.

On 11/8 with EWZ at $39.91 I closed the trade for a profit of $10.00 or about 2.43% over 41 days. Not my best trade for sure but, I did not lose any money.

Date		EXP	Strike	Price	Ct	C/P	Cost	Balance
09/28/18	SO	11/16/18	$40.00	$0.63	2	C	$126.00	$126.00
09/28/18	BO	11/16/18	$43.00	$0.19	2	C	-$42.00	$84.00
09/28/18	SO	11/16/18	$29.00	$0.77	2	P	$154.00	$238.00
09/28/18	BO	11/16/18	$26.00	$0.27	2	P	-$58.00	$180.00
11/8/18	BC	11/16/18	$40.00	$0.86	2	C	-$172.00	$8.00
11/08/18	SC	11/16/18	$43.00	$0.05	2	C	$10.00	$18.00
11/08/18	BC	11/16/18	$29.00	$0.01	2	P	-$9.00	$9.00
11/08/18	SC	11/16/18	$26.00	$0.01	2	P	$1.00	$10.00
							Profit of:	$10.00

NKE – 10/2/18 – Iron Condor

NKE had a big earnings Implied Volatility drop after earnings but still looked pretty good for an Iron Condor. I could have gotten more premium trading before earnings but there is a huge risk doing that, which is why you get more premium.

On 10/2 I sold the 11/16 $87.50 Call and purchased the $92.50 Call to cover. I also sold the $80.00 Put, purchasing the $75.00 Put to cover with NKE trading at $83.15. I was taking a little more risk to the downside based on the Delta of the short Put but felt it would work out.

The trade did not go well as NKE continued to fall. On 11/9 I found myself with a negative trade that I either needed to roll or close for a loss. I was going on a trip and had not planned to hold any trades on the 11/16 expiration since I would be gone. So … here I was.

On 11/14 with NKE trading at $75.20 I finally decided to close for a loss because I could not find a roll that I could get for a credit.

I closed after 43 days for a loss of $268.00 on an initial risk of $358.00 or 74.86%

Date		EXP	Strike	Price	Ct	C/P	Cost	Balance
10/2/18	SO	11/16/18	$87.50	$0.96	1	C	$96.00	$96.00
10/02/18	BO	11/16/18	$92.50	$0.26	1	C	-$26.00	$70.00
10/02/18	SO	11/16/18	$80.00	$1.00	1	P	$100.00	$170.00
10/02/18	BO	11/16/18	$75.00	$0.28	1	P	-$32.00	$138.00
11/14/18	BC	11/16/18	$87.50	$0.06	1	C	-$6.00	$132.00
11/14/18	SC	11/16/18	$92.50	$0.05	1	C	$5.00	$137.00
11/14/18	BC	11/16/18	$80.00	$4.04	1	P	-$404.00	-$267.00
11/14/18	SC	11/16/18	$75.00	$0.05	1	P	-$1.00	-$268.00
							Loss of:	-$268.00

COST – 10/8/18 – Iron Condor

I liked the price action on COST and was able to get a pretty good premium (or at least I initially though so) with Implied Volatility at 34.04 so I decided to go with an Iron Condor.

On 10/8 with COST trading at 223.27 I sold the 11/16 $240 Call and purchased the $250 Call. I also sold the $210 Put and purchased the $200 Put.

Remember above when I said I 'thought' I got a pretty good premium. Well, I forgot to take into account that the spread was $10.00 wide on this one. In actuality this was not a great trade for the risk.

My break even was $208.55 and $241.44 and I had a 68.68% chance of success.

On 11/12 after 39 days my GTC was hit and the trade closed for a $65.00 profit. This was a return of 7.56% because my risk was $860.00, this is what I meant by not really as good of a trade as I thought.

Date		EXP	Strike	Price	Ct	C/P	Cost	Balance
10/08/18	SO	11/16/18	$240.00	$0.77	1	C	$77.00	$77.00
10/08/18	BO	11/16/18	$250.00	$0.25	1	C	-$25.00	$52.00
10/08/18	SO	11/16/18	$210.00	$1.61	1	P	$161.00	$213.00
10/08/18	BO	11/16/18	$200.00	$0.69	1	P	-$73.00	$140.00
11/12/18	BC	11/16/18	$240.00	$0.68	1	C	-$68.00	$72.00
11/12/18	SC	11/16/18	$250.00	$0.04	1	C	$4.00	$76.00
11/12/18	BC	11/16/18	$210.00	$0.11	1	P	-$11.00	$65.00
11/12/18	SC	11/16/18	$200.00	$0.04	1	P	$0.00	$65.00
						Profit of:		$65.00

WMT – 10/12/18 Iron Condor

Normally you can count on WMT to trade in a relatively predictable manner, but not always which is what I ran into on this trade.

On 10/12 with WMT trading at $94.52 I decided to place an Iron Condor trade. I sold the 11/16 $100 Call and purchased the $105 Call. I completed the Iron Condor by selling the $85 Put and covering it with the $80 Put.

WMT had an Implied Volatility of 69.49 when I started the trade which was pretty high for WMT. My probability of success was 62.49% when I started the trade.

On 11/9 WMT was trading at $105.52 which put both my short and long Call in the money and me at a loss. I started working on a roll out for a couple of more weeks provided I could do it for a credit. After a lot of playing around with weeks and strikes I was finally able to roll out the position using the same strike to the 11/30 expiration.

Since I had the adjust the trade I moved my GTC order to break even to just close the trade and move on.

On 11/15 my GTC finally hit and I closed the trade for $1.00 or .27% over 34 days. WMT had moved back to $99.54 which enabled me to close. This time the probabilities with a little help from a roll made the trade work.

Ironically, if I had just waited to the 11/16 expiration instead of trying to roll this trade would have hit my initial GTC order and I would have made closer to 11% on this trade. Oh well, sometimes trading works out that way. You think you are doing the right thing but make it worse. Sometimes it is just better to let these types of Iron Condors play out win or lose.

Date		EXP	Strike	Price	Ct	C/P	Cost	Balance
10/12/18	SO	11/16/18	$100.00	$1.37	1	C	$137.00	$137.00
10/12/18	BO	11/16/18	$105.00	$0.48	1	C	-$48.00	$89.00
10/12/18	SO	11/16/18	$85.00	$0.71	1	P	$71.00	$160.00
10/12/18	B	11/16/18	$80.00	$0.30	1	P	-$34.00	$126.00

		O						
11/09/18	BC	11/16/18	$100.00	$6.29	1	C	-$629.00	-$503.00
11/09/18	SC	11/16/18	$105.00	$2.75	1	C	$275.00	-$228.00
11/09/18	SO	11/30/18	$100.00	$6.61	1	C	$661.00	$433.00
11/09/18	BO	11/30/18	$105.00	$3.12	1	C	-$316.00	$117.00
11/13/18	BC	11/16/18	$85.00	$0.35	1	P	-$35.00	$82.00
11/13/18	SC	11/16/18	$80.00	$0.40	1	P	$40.00	$122.00
11/13/18	SO	11/30/18	$90.00	$0.41	1	P	$41.00	$163.00
11/13/18	BO	11/30/18	$85.00	$0.36	1	P	-$40.00	$123.00
11/15/18	BC	11/30/18	$100.00	$1.29	1	C	-$129.00	-$6.00
11/15/18	SC	11/30/18	$105.00	$0.19	1	C	$19.00	$13.00
11/15/18	BC	11/30/18	$90.00	$0.14	1	P	-$18.00	-$5.00
11/15/18	SC	11/30/18	$85.00	$0.06	1	P	$6.00	$1.00
							Profit of:	$1.00

EEM – 10/12/18 – Iron Condor

This was a hedge trade I had on a Diagonal that was losing money. I wanted to try and take advantage of EEM moving into a sideways range after a move down and use that premium to help my Diagonal.

I entered this Iron Condor with EEM trading at 40.14, an Implied Volatility of 62.08 and a probability of success of 67.40% which meant this was a good Iron Condor even if there was no hedge. Sometimes I will skew my hedge Iron Condor's to protect my hedge, this trade however could have been traded on its own merit.

On 10/12 I sold the 11/16 $42 Call and purchased the $45 Call. I sold the $37 Put and purchased the $34 Put to cover. This gave me a $3.00 spread and a total risk of $490.00 with a potential profit of $110.00. My break even prices were $36.41 and $42.59.

On 11/1 after 20 days my GTC order hit and I closed this trade for a profit of $52.00 or about 10.61%. Not as good as I prefer but as a hedge it was fine.

Date		EXP	Strike	Price	Ct	C/P	Cost	Balance
10/12/18	SO	11/16/18	$42.00	$0.44	2	C	$88.00	$88.00
10/12/18	BO	11/16/18	$45.00	$0.05	2	C	-$10.00	$78.00
10/12/18	SO	11/16/18	$37.00	$0.29	2	P	$58.00	$136.00
10/12/18	BO	11/16/18	$34.00	$0.09	2	P	-$26.00	$110.00
11/11/18	BC	11/16/18	$42.00	$0.10	2	C	-$20.00	$90.00
11/11/18	SC	11/16/18	$45.00	$0.01	2	C	$2.00	$92.00
11/11/18	BC	11/16/18	$37.00	$0.17	2	P	-$42.00	$50.00
11/11/18	SC	11/16/18	$34.00	$0.01	2	P	$2.00	$52.00
							Profit of:	$52.00

XOP – 10/18/18 – Iron Condor

XOP is another security I like to trade because it is somewhat predictable. That is, unless it is not. This trade went bad pretty quickly, just bad luck really, I got in at the worst time and once it started to move against me I decided to hold and play the probabilities. They did not work out this time.

On 10/18 with XOP trading at $40.38 I entered into an Iron Condor expecting XOP to say within a range. I sold the 11/23 $44 Call and purchased the $47 Call. I sold the $38 Put and purchased the $35

Put.

Implied Volatility was at 43.03 and looked to be going down which was another plus for me on this trade. My initial probability for success was 62.56%.

As I said, this trade just did not work out. On 11/19 with XOP trading below my short AND long Puts I was assigned on my short Put. Being this far in the money there was really no sense in even looking for a roll, especially since I had already been assigned. I sold my assigned long stock position and sold my long Put to close out the trade.

I just let my Calls expire, not sense paying commissions to close them since they were so far out of the money.

I ended up with a loss of $230.00 on a risk of about $230.00 or 100%. I was in this trade for 36 days.

Date		EXP	Strike	Price	Ct	C/P	Cost	Balance
10/18/18	SO	11/23/18	$44.00	$0.36	1	C	$36.00	$36.00
10/18/18	BO	11/23/18	$47.00	$0.06	1	C	-$6.00	$30.00
10/18/18	SO	11/23/18	$38.00	$0.66	1	P	$66.00	$96.00
10/18/18	BO	11/23/18	$35.00	$0.27	1	P	-$27.00	$69.00
11/19/18	AS	Assigned			200		-$3,800.00	-$3,731.00
11/20/18		Sold	Shares	$32.90	200		$3,298.00	-$433.00
11/20/18		11/23/18	$35.00	$2.04			$203.00	-$203.00
							Loss of:	-$230.00

V – 10/25/18 – Iron Condor

This was another hedge trade that I did to offset some losses I was showing on a Diagonal I had on.

On 10/25 with V trading at $139.69 I placed an Iron Condor to take advantage of V if it stayed range bound as part of my Diagonal hedge. I sold the 11/30 $145 Call and covered it with the $149 Call. I sold the $124 Put and covered it with the $120 Put for a credit of $1.25.

My GTC order was hit on 11/19 after 25 days giving me a profit of $61.00 on a risk of $279.00 or 21.86% which was a very good return. When I entered the trade V had an Implied Volatility of 42.1 which enabled me to get a good premium. Because this was a hedge I also picked my short Call a little closer than normal. Still this traded started out with a 62.9% chance of success.

Date		EXP	Strike	Price	Ct	C/P	Cost	Balance
10/25/18	SO	11/30/18	$145.00	$1.88	1	C	$188.00	$188.00
10/25/18	BO	11/30/18	$149.00	$0.82	1	C	-$82.00	$106.00
10/25/18	SO	11/30/18	$124.00	$0.85	1	P	$85.00	$191.00
10/25/18	BO	11/30/18	$120.00	$0.66	1	P	-$70.00	$121.00
11/19/18	BC	11/30/18	$145.00	$0.62	1	C	-$62.00	$59.00
11/19/18	SC	11/30/18	$149.00	$0.10	1	C	$10.00	$69.00
11/19/18	BC	11/30/18	$124.00	$0.18	1	P	-$18.00	$51.00
11/19/18	SC	11/30/18	$120.00	$0.14	1	P	$10.00	$61.00
							Profit of:	$61.00

EMR – 11/9/18 – Iron Condor

On 11/9 with EMR trading at $68.31 I entered into an Iron Condor position by selling the 12/21 $72.50 Call and purchasing he $75.00 Call. I also sold the $65.00 Put and purchased the $60.00 Put to cover it.

I actually entered this trade as a hedge to an ongoing Diagonal I was struggling to make a profit on. This trade had more risk to the downside because of the $5.00 spread on the Puts as opposed to the $2.50 spread on the Calls. In retrospect I probably made a mistake there but the way the market had been springing up and down I decided to go with it.

When I entered the trade EMR implied volatility was at 50.48 and the trade had a probability of success of 55.51%. Of course, if I was threatened on the upside at least my Diagonal would be helping this trade out.

My GTC order was hit on 12/3 after 24 days for a profit of $42.00 on a risk of $395.00 or 10.63%. Not too bad for a hedge trade.

Date		EXP	Strike	Price	Ct	C/P	Cost	Balance
11/09/18	SO	12/21/18	$72.50	$0.55	1	C	$55.00	$55.00
11/09/18	BO	12/21/18	$75.00	$0.20	1	C	-$20.00	$35.00
11/09/18	SO	12/21/18	$65.00	$1.10	1	P	$110.00	$145.00
11/09/18	BO	12/21/18	$60.00	$0.40	1	P	-$44.00	$101.00
12/03/18	BC	12/21/18	$72.50	$0.05	1	C	-$5.00	$96.00
12/03/18	SC	12/21/18	$75.00	$0.14	1	C	$14.00	$110.00
12/03/18	BC	12/21/18	$65.00	$0.65	1	P	-$65.00	$45.00
12/03/18	SC	12/21/18	$60.00	$0.01	1	P	-$3.00	$42.00
							Profit of:	$42.00

CAT – 11/28/18 – Iron Condor

CAT has been good to me in the past trading different types of Condors so I always take a look at it to see if there is enough premium to trade.

On 11/28 I was able to get a good premium on an Iron Condor primarily because Implied Volatility was at 82.41 which was pretty high for CAT. I sold the 1/18/19 $145 Call and purchased the $150 Call. I sold the $115 Put and purchased the $110 Put. I was able to get a credit of $1.32 on a risk of $3.68 per contract. I set my GTC at about $.70.

When I started the trade it showed about a 62.06% of profitability if I held to expiration.

CAT had been at a loss or small gain for the majority of the trade so on 12/31 when I saw I could close it for $.74 I decided to go ahead and take my profit and move on. I had some losses on these trades over the past few months so wanted to take advantage of a chance to get out at close to my goal before the market dropped again.

I closed the trade for a $50.00 profit on a risk of $368.00 or 13.59% after 33 days. A good return. CAT was at $126.86 when I closed the trade and Implied Volatility had dropped to 67.86.

Date		EXP	Strike	Price	Ct	C/P	Cost	Balance
11/28/18	SO	01/18/19	$145.00	$1.46	1	C	$146.00	$146.00
11/28/18	BO	01/18/19	$150.00	$0.81	1	C	-$81.00	$65.00
11/28/18	SO	01/18/19	$115.00	$1.87	1	P	$187.00	$252.00
11/28/18	BO	01/18/19	$110.00	$1.20	1	P	-$124.00	$128.00
12/31/18	BC	01/18/19	$145.00	$0.24	1	C	-$24.00	$104.00
12/31/18	SC	01/18/19	$150.00	$0.12	1	C	$12.00	$116.00
12/31/18	BC	01/18/19	$115.00	$1.28	1	P	-$132.00	-$16.00
12/31/18	SC	01/18/19	$110.00	$0.66	1	P	$66.00	$50.00
							Profit of:	$50.00

V – 11/29/18 – Iron Condor

Seems like I am always trading V. I found a decent premium on this Iron Condor even though Implied Volatility was only at 32.49. It actually went up to 54.82 by the time the trade closed which meant I had to hold on to this one longer to wait on time decay to make me money.

On 11/29 I sold the 1/18/19 $150 Call and purchased the $155 Call. I sold the $125 Put and purchased the $120 Put. I got a $1.08 credit (not great) on a risk of $3.92.

When I entered the trade V was trading at $139.51, during the course of the trade it dropped to $133.31 by the time my GTC order hit. This caused Implied Volatility to spike but at least it stayed above my short Put at $125. The initial probably of success for this trade was 69.25% which is why I was still able to close for a profit even though V dropped quite a bit. I also allowed more room to the downside because of recent market activity.

On 01/02/19 my GTC hit and I closed the trade for a $46.00 profit over 34 days. My risk was $392.00 so my return was 11.73%.

Date		EXP	Strike	Price	Ct	C/P	Cost	Balance
11/29/18	SO	01/18/19	$150.00	$1.13	1	C	$113.00	$113.00
11/29/18	BO	01/18/19	$155.00	$0.41	1	C	-$41.00	$72.00
11/29/18	SO	01/18/19	$125.00	$1.04	1	P	$104.00	$176.00
11/29/18	BO	01/18/19	$120.00	$0.68	1	P	-$72.00	104
01/02/19	BC	01/18/19	$150.00	$0.06	1	C	-$6.00	$98.00
01/02/19	SC	01/18/19	$155.00	$0.01	1	C	$1.00	$99.00
01/02/19	BC	01/18/19	$125.00	$0.90	1	P	-$90.00	$9.00

01/02/19	SC	01/18/19	$120.00	$0.41	1	P	$37.00	$46.00
						Profit of:	$46.00

GS – 12/04/18 – Iron Condor

We found a pretty good Iron Condor trade with GS trading at $184.94 an Implied Volatility of 83.84 and a trade probability of success of about 61%.

On 12/04 we sold the 1/18/19 $205 Call and purchased the $210 Call. We sold the $170 Put and purchased the $165 Put to cover. We brought in an initial credit of $1.40 and set our GTC at $.75.

We opened the day on 11/11/19 showing a $42.00 profit and promptly watched it disappear. By the end of the day it had moved back up to $32.00 with GS trading at $176.04. We decided to take the money and run! Expiration was the following week so probably a good decision.

After 38 days we ended up with a profit of $32.00 or 8.79%. Time to move on to the next trade.

Date		EXP	Strike	Price	Ct	C/P	Cost	Balance
12/04/18	SO	01/18/19	$205.00	$1.46	1	C	$146.00	$146.00
12/04/18	BO	01/18/19	$210.00	$0.88	1	C	-$88.00	$58.00
12/04/18	SO	01/18/19	$170.00	$2.69	1	P	$269.00	$327.00
12/04/18	BO	01/18/19	$165.00	$1.87	1	P	-$191.00	136
01/11/19	BC	01/18/19	$205.00	$0.07	1	C	-$7.00	$129.00
01/11/19	SC	01/18/19	$210.00	$0.02	1	C	$2.00	$131.00
01/11/19	BC	01/18/19	$170.00	$1.83	1	P	-$187.00	-$56.00
01/11/19	S	01/18/19	$165.00	$0.88	1	P	$88.00	$32.00

	C						
						Profit of:	$32.00

Chapter 4

Broken Wing Iron Condors – Non Index

A broken wing iron condor is just an iron condor with a that does not have the same spread between the Calls and Puts.

These trades would typically not have any risk to the 'wing' that has the smaller spread. All the risk would be to the side with the larger wing if you set them up correctly. This means your credit must be larger than your shorter spread.

If you sold a broken wing iron condor with by shorting a 300 Call and buying a $305 Call and shorting a $280 put and buying a $278 you need a credit of greater than $280-$278 or $2.00 if you want no risk to the downside.

The rules we follow are almost the same as in Chapter 3. The main difference is that:

We set our GTC at about 35% to 40% of our credit instead of about 50%. We do this because we are getting a much larger credit for the risk we are taking.

Sometimes you may also see us trade these as part of a swing trade strategy. We use different closing rules for those and do not go into them here, but you may see them on our website, Facebook or Twitter feeds.

EWZ – 9/04/18 – Broken Wing Iron Condor

I took this trade out the same day I did the EWZ trade above. I traded it as a comparison to different strategies and risk/reward expectations.

Both trades were profitable (this time) I typically don't trade the same security with two different strategies at the same time unless it is some kind of hedge trade. I did it this time just for you and this book.

When I entered this trade on 9/4 as a Broken Wind Iron Condor I traded it so that I had no upside risk and my downside break even as at $29.03. Remember a Broken Wind Iron Condor is somewhat of a directional play as compared to a regular Iron Condor.

Everything went very well and on 9/21 my GTC order was hit and the position closed. My overall risk was $406.00 and my max profit would have been $394.00 if I held to the end, which I don't usually do. Instead I closed early for a profit of $144.00 or 35.47% over 17 days. Wish all my trades worked out this well!

Date		EXP	Strike	Price	Ct	C/P	Cost	Balance
09/04/18	SO	10/19/18	$31.00	$2.46	2	C	$492.00	$492.00
09/04/18	BO	10/19/18	$32.00	$2.00	2	C	-$400.00	$92.00
09/04/18	SO	10/19/18	$31.00	$2.28	2	P	$456.00	$548.00
09/04/18	BO	10/19/18	$27.00	$0.77	2	P	-$154.00	$394.00
09/21/18	BC	10/19/18	$31.00	$3.50	2	C	-$700.00	-$306.00
09/21/18	SC	10/19/18	$32.00	$2.78	2	C	$556.00	$250.00
09/21/18	BC	10/19/18	$31.00	$0.60	2	P	-$120.00	$130.00
09/21/18	SC	10/19/18	$27.00	$0.07	2	P	$14.00	$144.00
							Profit of:	$144.00

AMAT – 9/10/18 – Broken Wing Iron Condor

On 9/10 AMAT had moved down to what I really felt would be a good support area so I decided to enter a Broken Wing Iron Condor figuring this trade would head back up.

Because I entered this trade at about a $1.43 credit, since my

Calls were 1 point away that meant that if AMAT finished anywhere above $40.00 the least I would make if held to expiration was $43.00.

With AMAT trading at $39.54 I sold the 10/19 $40 Call and purchased the $41 Call to cover it. I also sold the 10/19 $39 Put and purchased the $34 Put to finish out my Broken Wing Iron Condor. My credit was $143.00 and based on my $5.00 Put spread my risk was $357.00 to the downside and none to the upside.

If we held to expiration we would want this trade to close between $39 and $40 for a max profit of $143.00 but since we always put in a GTC order I wanted to try for about a $50.00 profit at any point during this trade. Initially, this trade was showing a 67% probability of success.

Almost from the beginning this trade did not cooperate with me and was showing a loss most of the time. On 10/2 it had a pretty big up day which gave me the opportunity to close for a profit, so I took it.

I ended up with a $26.00 profit after 22 days on my risk of $357.00 which is a 7.28% return.

I closed this position with AMAT trading at $39.14.

Date		EXP	Strike	Price	Ct	C/P	Cost	Balance
09/10/18	SO	10/19/18	$40.00	$1.47	1	C	$147.00	$147.00
09/10/18	BO	10/19/18	$41.00	$1.05	1	C	-$105.00	$42.00
09/10/18	SO	10/19/18	$39.00	$1.26	1	P	$126.00	$168.00
09/10/18	BO	10/19/18	$34.00	$0.21	1	P	-$25.00	$143.00
10/02/18	BC	10/19/18	$40.00	$0.67	1	C	-$67.00	$76.00
10/02/18	SC	10/19/18	$41.00	$0.35	1	C	$35.00	$111.00
10/02/18	BC	10/19/18	$39.00	$0.86	1	P	-$90.00	$21.00
10/02/18	S	10/19/18	$34.00	$0.05	1	P	$5.00	$26.00

	C						
						Profit of:	$26.00

INTC – 9/11/18 – Broken Wing Iron Condor

Entered this trade on 9/11 with no upside risk thinking there would be more chance of a move up after a hard move down. Implied Volatility was 46 and I was showing a 64.20% probability of success.

This was a counter trend or contrarian bet that INTC would not continue down without finding buyers willing to get in at a steep discount.

The overall market made some major moves down so I moved my initial GTC order up to try and get out of this trade with as much profit as possible.

When I entered this trade I had a risk of $88.00 and a potential profit of $112.00. I closed the trade on 10/15 for a profit of $22.00 or about 25% over 34 days.

Date		EXP	Strike	Price	Ct	C/P	Cost	Balance
09/11/18	SO	10/19/18	$45.00	$1.75	1	C	$175.00	$175.00
09/11/18	BO	10/19/18	$46.00	$1.22	1	C	-$122.00	$53.00
09/11/18	SO	10/19/18	$45.00	$1.14	1	P	$114.00	$167.00
09/11/18	BO	10/19/18	$43.00	$0.55	1	P	-$55.00	$112.00
10/15/18	BC	10/19/18	$45.00	$0.72	1	C	-$72.00	$40.00
10/15/18	SC	10/19/18	$46.00	$0.28	1	C	$28.00	$68.00
10/15/18	BC	10/19/18	$45.00	$0.60	1	P	-$60.00	$8.00

10/15/18	SC	10/19/18	$43.00	$0.14	1	P	$14.00	$22.00
						Profit of:		$22.00

V – 9/13/18 – Broken Wind Iron Condor

This was part of a series of trades I did in V working different strategies to take advantage of V's run up to highs and pull back. I felt there was more downward pressure and it would be difficult for V to break to new highs over the course of this trade.

I entered this trade with V at 147.29 with no downside risk and a break even on the upside of $153.69 which would have been a new 52 week high.

The implied volatility when I entered the trade was 15.88 and I was showing a 74% chance of a successful trade if held until expiration. My risk was $390.00 and my max profit would have been $360.00 in a perfect world but I only wanted about a third of that when I set my GTC order.

I sold the 10/26 $152.50 Call while purchasing the $155.00 Call. On the Put side I sold the $150.00 Put and purchased the $149.00 Put.

On 10/8 after 25 days my GTC order was hit and I closed this trade for a $120.00 profit or 30.77%. I wish I had these types of trades everyday.

Date		EXP	Strike	Price	Ct	C/P	Cost	Balance
09/13/18	SO	10/26/18	$152.50	$1.74	3	C	$522.00	$522.00
09/13/18	BO	10/26/18	$155.00	$1.09	3	C	-$327.00	$195.00
09/13/18	SO	10/26/18	$150.00	$5.00	3	P	$1,500.00	$1,695.00
09/13/18	BO	10/26/18	$149.00	$4.45	3	P	-$1,335.00	$360.00
10/08/18	B	10/26/18	$152.50	$0.61	3	C	-$183.00	$177.00

		C						
10/08/18		SC	10/26/18	$155.00	$0.31	3	C	$93.00	$270.00
10/08/18		BC	10/26/18	$150.00	$6.85	3	P	-$2,055.00	-$1,785.00
10/08/18		SC	10/26/18	$149.00	$6.35	3	P	$1,905.00	$120.00
							Profit of:	$120.00

EEM – 9/14/18 – Broken Wind Iron Condor

On 9/14 EEM was trading at $41.99 and I decided to take a trade with no downside risk because if a Diagonal trade I had that was showing a loss. This was a hedge trade to protect my Diagonal to the downside.

I sold the 10/26 $42 Call and purchased the $45 Call. I sold the $42 Put and bought the $41 Put to finish out the Broken Wing Iron Condor. My max loss would be $338 and my break even to the upside was $43.31.

Just looking at this on its own merit I had a 68.27% probability of success if held to the expiration.

I closed this trade on 10/12 for a profit of $64.00 which went to offset some of my open loss on the Diagonal. This was a profit of 18.93% over 28 days.

Date		EXP	Strike	Price	Ct	C/P	Cost	Balance
09/14/18	SO	10/26/18	$42.00	$1.14	2	C	$228.00	$228.00
09/14/18	BO	10/26/18	$45.00	$0.18	2	C	-$36.00	$192.00
09/14/18	SO	10/26/18	$42.00	$1.01	2	P	$202.00	$394.00
09/14/18	BO	10/26/18	$41.00	$0.66	2	P	-$140.00	$254.00
10/12/18	BC	10/26/18	$42.00	$0.15	2	C	-$30.00	$224.00

10/12/18	SC	10/26/18	$45.00	$0.01	2	C	$2.00	$226.00
10/12/18	BC	10/26/18	$42.00	$1.98	2	P	-$396.00	-$170.00
10/12/18	SC	10/26/18	$41.00	$1.21	2	P	$234.00	$64.00
							Profit of:	$64.00

XOP – 9/24/18 – Broken Wing Iron Condor

XOP was trading at $43.22 and I thought a move down or a sideways move was the most likely outcome over the next month or so. I entered this trade with no downside risk and an upside break even of $45.57.

When I entered this one Implied Volatility was at 13.40 and moving down which is good. It was also showing a 71.7% probability of success.

I sold the 11/16 $44 Call and purchased the $48 Call. I sold the $44 Put and bought the $43 Put. My max risk was $486.00 with a max profit potential of $306.00. I set a GTC order to keep about $80.00 of the potential.

On 10/11 XOP was down big at $41.16 and my trade was showing a profit. Probability of success is now 82%.

On 10/18 my GTC order hit as XOP was bouncing off of a bottom and moving back up.

I closed for a profit of $78.00 or 16.05% over 24 days.

Date		EXP	Strike	Price	Ct	C/P	Cost	Balance
09/24/18	SO	11/16/18	$44.00	$1.37	2	C	$274.00	$274.00
09/24/18	BO	11/16/18	$48.00	$0.29	2	C	-$58.00	$216.00
09/24/18	SO	11/16/18	$44.00	$2.05	2	P	$410.00	$626.00

09/24/18	BO	11/16/18	$43.00	$1.56	2	P	-$320.00	$306.00
10/18/18	BC	11/16/18	$44.00	$0.32	2	C	-$64.00	$242.00
10/18/18	SC	11/16/18	$48.00	$0.07	2	C	$14.00	$256.00
10/18/18	BC	11/16/18	$44.00	$3.74	2	P	-$748.00	-$492.00
10/18/18	SC	11/16/18	$43.00	$2.89	2	P	$570.00	$78.00
						Profit of:	$78.00

IYR – 09/24/18 – Broken Wing Condor

I decided to place a Broken Wing Condor in IYR after a move down with no risk to the upside. I felt it had its run down and now was due for a rebound. Turns out I was wrong, that is the problem with trying to pick a direction.

With IYR trading at $80.71 I sold the 11/16 $80 Call and purchased the $81 Call. I sold the $80 Put and purchased the $76 Put to cover my long Put. My risk was about $500.00 with a potential max profit of $292.00 if held to expiration and the security finished at the optimal price of $80.11. Implied volatility was at 28.67 but appeared to be rising, if I was right about the price moving back up then the implied volatility would start to go down which is what I would prefer.

As I stated above, turns out I was wrong and the security starting a move up. I had varying degrees of loss for almost the entire trade. On 11/5 with a move up in IYR I decided to take advantage of the move and close the position with IYR trading at $78.71.

I ended up with a loss of $52.00 or about 10.4%. Based on my rules I probably should have just let this trade play out, but sometimes I don't follow my own rules. Trading is a little science and a little art.

The best reason I can give you for why I did not follow my own rules is two part. One, this trade had been at a much greater loss and had not preformed well from the beginning. Two, I had been in this trade for 42 days which is a long time for these. It was time to close.

Date		EXP	Strike	Price	Ct	C/P	Cost	Balance
09/24/18	SO	11/16/18	$80.00	$1.60	2	C	$320.00	$320.00
09/24/18	BO	11/16/18	$81.00	$1.04	2	C	-$208.00	$112.00
09/24/18	SO	11/16/18	$80.00	$1.45	2	P	$290.00	$402.00
09/24/18	BO	11/16/18	$76.00	$0.51	2	P	-$110.00	$292.00
11/05/18	BC	11/16/18	$80.00	$0.49	2	C	-$98.00	$194.00
11/05/18	SC	11/16/18	$81.00	$0.22	2	C	$44.00	$238.00
11/05/18	BC	11/16/18	$80.00	$1.76	2	P	-$352.00	-$114.00
11/05/18	SC	11/16/18	$76.00	$0.35	2	P	$62.00	-$52.00
							Profit of:	-$52.00

TLT – 09/25/18 – Broken Wing Iron Condor

I got in a little bit of a habit of placing these Broken Wing Iron Condors during this time period. Great if you are expecting the market to move a certain direction, but don't over do them. If the market suddenly changes on you and you are playing the directional game you will get burned fast.

On 9/25 I entered this trade with no upside risk. My break even was at $133.74, Implied Volatility was at 24.8 and looked to be rising. It showed an almost 73% probability of success; I set my GTC to keep about half of my potential profit.

Just 2 days later my GTC order hit and I closed the trade for a $59.00 profit or about 15.69%. Yes, and in just 2 DAYS!

Date	EXP	Strike	Price	Ct	C/P	Cost	Balance

09/25/18	SO	11/16/18	$117.00	$1.38	1	C	$138.00	$138.00
09/25/18	BO	11/16/18	$118.00	$0.97	1	C	-$97.00	$41.00
09/25/18	SO	11/16/18	$115.00	$1.09	1	P	$109.00	$150.00
09/25/18	BO	11/16/18	$110.00	$0.22	1	P	-$26.00	$124.00
9/27/18	BC	11/16/18	$117.00	$1.55	1	C	-$155.00	-$31.00
09/27/18	SC	11/16/18	$118.00	$1.35	1	C	$135.00	$104.00
09/27/18	BC	11/16/18	$115.00	$0.63	1	P	-$63.00	$41.00
09/27/18	SC	11/16/18	$110.00	$0.22	1	P	$22.00	$59.00
						Profit of:	$59.00

TLT – 10/2/18 – Broken Wing Iron Condor

I started this trade with TLT trading at $116.98 and took a no upside risk trade using the Broken Wing Iron Condor strategy. TLT however did not cooperate.

On 10/2 I sold the 11/16 $115 Call and purchased the $116 Call. I also sold the $115 Put and purchased the $110 Put to cover. I started out with a credit of $124.00 (also max profit) on a risk of $372.00 and set my usual GTC order.

On 11/8 TLT was trading at $112.64 so I started looking for an opportunity to roll the trade out a couple of more weeks from 11/16 to 11/30 expiration. I was able to find a credit trade that let me keep the same strikes and get about 2 more weeks for the trade to move to profitability.

One thing I typically do when I have to roll a Condor is set my GTC at break even to just get out of the trade. If I am having to defend, things have obviously gone wrong so I usually prefer to close as soon as possible and move on to another trade.

On 11/20 after 49 total days my break even GTC order hit and I was able to get out of the trade for a very small profit of $5.00 or 1.34% on my initial $372.00 risk.

Date		EXP	Strike	Price	Ct	C/P	Cost	Balance
10/2/18	SO	11/16/18	$115.00	$2.86	1	C	$286.00	$286.00
10/02/18	BO	11/16/18	$116.00	$2.16	1	C	-$216.00	$70.00
10/02/18	SO	11/16/18	$115.00	$0.71	1	P	$71.00	$141.00
10/02/18	BO	11/16/18	$110.00	$0.13	1	P	-$17.00	$124.00
11/08/18	BC	11/16/18	$115.00	$2.37	1	P	-$237.00	-$113.00
11/08/18	SC	11/16/18	$110.00	$0.06	1	P	$6.00	-$107.00
11/08/18	SO	11/30/18	$115.00	$2.48	1	P	$248.00	$141.00
11/08/18	BO	11/30/18	$110.00	$0.21	1	P	-$25.00	$116.00
11/08/18	BC	11/16/18	$115.00	$0.07	1	C	-$7.00	$109.00
11/08/18	SC	11/16/18	$116.00	$0.03	1	C	$3.00	$112.00
11/08/18	SO	11/30/18	$115.00	$0.25	1	C	$25.00	$137.00
11/08/18	BO	11/30/18	$116.00	$0.14	1	C	-$18.00	$119.00
11/20/18	BC	11/30/18	$115.00	$0.96	1	C	-$96.00	$23.00
11/20/18	SC	11/30/18	$116.00	$0.48	1	C	$48.00	$71.00
11/20/18	BC	11/30/18	$115.00	$0.66	1	P	-$70.00	$1.00
11/20/18	SC	11/30/18	$110.00	$0.04	1	P	$4.00	$5.00
							Profit of:	$5.00

FXE – 10/3/18 – Broken Wing Iron Condor

When I can find opportunities I like to trade FXE because it trends well. Finding premium can be a challenge, however.

On 10/3 with FXE trading at $110.26 and Implied Volatility at 54.75 I was able to get into a Broken Wind Iron Condor with no upside risk and a probability of success of about 73.26%. My breakeven on the down side was at $108.70.

I sold the 11/16 $110 Call and purchased the $111 Call while selling the $110 Put and buying the $106 Put to cover it for a credit of $1.28. My risk was $272.00 to the downside, and $0.00 to the upside. I put in a GTC order for $.62 and waited.

FXE did not cooperate with my great plans to make money. It moved down consistently showing losses on the trade. On 11/8 I got a spike up so after 36 days I decided to close the trade for small profit.

I made $18.00 on my $272.00 risk or about 6.62%.

Date		EXP	Strike	Price	Ct	C/P	Cost	Balance
10/03/18	SO	11/16/18	$110.00	$1.44	1	C	$144.00	$144.00
10/03/18	BO	11/16/18	$111.00	$0.93	1	C	-$93.00	$51.00
10/03/18	SO	11/16/18	$110.00	$0.93	1	P	$93.00	$144.00
10/03/18	BO	11/16/18	$106.00	$0.16	1	P	-$20.00	$124.00
11/8/18	BC	11/16/18	$110.00	$0.25	1	C	-$25.00	$99.00
11/08/18	SC	11/16/18	$111.00	$0.05	1	C	$5.00	$104.00
11/08/18	BC	11/16/18	$110.00	$0.83	1	P	-$83.00	$21.00
11/08/18	SC	11/16/18	$106.00	$0.01	1	P	-$3.00	$22.00
							Profit of:	$18.00

MU – 10/18/18 – Broken Wing Iron Condor

I trade MU from time to time so I keep and eye on its price action. I felt it had pulled back a little and now was more likely to continue an upward move or at the very least stay in a range.

With MU trading at $41.68 I decided to enter a Broken Wing Iron Condor with no upside risk. The implied volatility was at 23.24 which actually went up over the trade instead of down. My probably of success was 64.15% if held to expiration, which of course I was not going to do.

On 11/8 my GTC order was hit and I closed the order for a $77.00 profit or about 15.28% on a $504.00 risk. My max profit was $296.00 if everything worked out perfect.

Date		EXP	Strike	Price	Ct	C/P	Cost	Balance
10/18/18	SO	11/16/18	$42.00	$1.84	2	C	$368.00	$368.00
10/18/18	BO	11/16/18	$43.00	$1.40	2	C	-$280.00	$88.00
10/18/18	SO	11/16/18	$41.00	$1.55	2	P	$310.00	$398.00
10/18/18	BO	11/16/18	$37.00	$0.47	2	P	-$102.00	$296.00
11/08/18	BC	11/16/18	$42.00	$0.69	2	C	-$138.00	$158.00
11/08/18	SC	11/16/18	$43.00	$0.36	2	C	$72.00	$230.00
11/08/18	BC	11/16/18	$41.00	$0.86	2	P	-$172.00	$58.00
11/08/18	SC	11/16/18	$37.00	$0.09	2	P	$19.00	$77.00
							Profit of:	$77.00

IYR – 11/5/18 – Broken Wing Iron Condor

After watching the market fall as a whole I felt there was good opportunity in a IYR Broken Wing Iron Condor with no upside risk. On

11/5 with IYR trading at $78.85 I sold the 12/21 $78 Call and purchased the $79 Call to cover. I then sold the $78 Put and Purchased the $74 Put to cover.

If I held to expiration my maximum profit could have been about $170.00 on a risk of $226.00. IYR Implied Volatility was 60.16 and the trade had a profitability probability of 66.18%. My estimated break even at expiration on this trade was at $76.26.

On 12/3 after 28 days my GTC order it and I made $48.00 on my risk of $226.00 or about 21.24% which was a very good return on this type of trade.

Date		EXP	Strike	Price	Ct	C/P	Cost	Balance
11/05/18	SO	12/21/18	$78.00	$2.36	1	C	$236.00	$236.00
11/05/18	BO	12/21/18	$79.00	$1.72	1	C	-$172.00	$64.00
11/05/18	SO	12/21/18	$78.00	$1.85	1	P	$185.00	$249.00
11/05/18	BO	12/21/18	$74.00	$0.75	1	P	-$79.00	$170.00
12/03/18	BC	12/21/18	$78.00	$3.76	1	C	-$376.00	-$206.00
12/03/18	SC	12/21/18	$79.00	$2.80	1	C	$280.00	$74.00
12/03/18	BC	12/21/18	$78.00	$0.24	1	P	-$24.00	$50.00
12/03/18	SC	12/21/18	$74.00	$0.02	1	P	-$2.00	$48.00
							Profit of:	$48.00

XLE – 12/11/18 – Broken Wind Iron Condor

I was able to find decent premium in XLE on 12/11. With XLE trading at $63.37 I decided to take a Broken Wind Iron Condor with no upside risk. My thought was the market was more likely to rebound from here. The advantage of these types of trades is that even if you turn out to be wrong you still might not lose money as opposed to a debit spread.

On 12/11 I sold the 1/18/19 $64 Call and purchased the $65 Call. I sold the $61 Put and bought the $56 Put. I had a pretty good range for profit and still got a good premium on this trade.

When I entered the trade XLE had an Implied Volatility of 84.25 and the trade had a 71.81% chance of profitability. I set my GTC order at $.83 which would leave me a small profit if it hit.

By 1/7/19 I was pretty frustrated with this trade. XLE was trading at 60.87 which was actually below my short Put. This trade had been at a loss for a while, so when I saw I could get out close to break even I decided to take advantage of it and close the trade.

I made a profit of $6.00 on a risk of $357.00 or 1.68% after 27 days. Not very good but I was just glad to get out of it.

Date		EXP	Strike	Price	Ct	C/P	Cost	Balance
12/11/18	SO	01/18/19	$64.00	$1.75	1	C	$175.00	$175.00
12/11/18	BO	01/18/19	$65.00	$1.33	1	C	-$133.00	$42.00
12/11/18	SO	01/18/19	$61.00	$1.55	1	P	$155.00	$197.00
12/11/18	BO	01/18/19	$56.00	$0.50	1	P	-$54.00	143
01/07/19	BC	01/18/19	$64.00	$0.24	1	C	-$24.00	$119.00
01/07/19	SC	01/18/19	$65.00	$0.12	1	C	$12.00	$131.00
01/07/19	BC	01/18/19	$61.00	$1.36	1	P	-$136.00	-$5.00
01/07/19	SC	01/18/19	$56.00	$0.15	1	P	$11.00	$6.00
							Profit of:	$6.00

KRE – 12/12/18 – Broken Wing Iron Condor

The market had gotten a little more volatile than I preferred for my range bound strategies. Yes, we need volatility to make money selling options but even to much of a good thing can be bad.

On 12/12 with KRE trading at $51.15 we decided to enter a broken wing iron condor in KRE with no up side risk. We felt it was about time for the market to rebound at least some.

We sold the 1/18/19 $53 Call and purchased the $54 Call. We sold the $49 Put and purchased the $44 Put for $1.06 credit. Volatility was at 69.14 when we entered the trade.

We set a GTC order for $.52.

On 1/10/19 we decided to go ahead and close the trade for $.57 instead of waiting for our GTC order to hit. Truthfully we just wanted to lock in some profit, probably could have waited but the market had been a little rough on us lately.

After 29 days we closed for a profit of $45.00 or 11.42%.

Date		EXP	Strike	Price	Ct	C/P	Cost	Balance
12/12/18	SO	01/18/19	$53.00	$0.90	1	C	$90.00	$90.00
12/12/18	BO	01/18/19	$54.00	$0.61	1	C	-$62.00	$28.00
12/12/18	SO	01/18/19	$49.00	$1.04	1	P	$104.00	$132.00
12/12/18	BO	01/18/19	$44.00	$0.25	1	P	-$26.00	106
01/10/19	BC	01/18/19	$53.00	$0.06	1	C	-$6.00	$100.00
01/10/19	SC	01/18/19	$54.00	$0.02	1	C	$2.00	$102.00
01/10/19	BC	01/18/19	$49.00	$0.58	1	P	-$58.00	$44.00
01/10/19	SC	01/18/19	$44.00	$0.05	1	P	$1.00	$45.00
							Profit of:	$45.00

TLT – 1/11/19 – Broken Wing Iron Condor

On 1/11 with TLT trading at $121.13 we felt there was a higher likely hood TLT would move down as opposed to making a substantial up more. We were able to get some good premium at a level we were comfortable with so we entered this broken wing iron condor.

Using the 3/15 expiration options we sold the $124 Call, bought the $129 Call, sold the $121 Put and bought the $120 Put for a credit of $1.12. We had not risk to the downside, all our risk was if TLT finished above $125.12.

We entered a GTC order for $.50 and waited. On 2/20 with TLT trading at $121.96 we decided to go ahead and close this trade for a profit of $41.00 or 10.46% over 40 days.

Date		EXP	Strike	Price	Ct	C/P	Cost	Balance
01/11/19	SO	3/15/19	$124.00	$0.92	1	C	$92.00	$92.00
01/11/19	BO	03/15/19	$129.00	$0.28	1	C	-$28.00	$64.00
01/11/19	SO	03/15/19	$121.00	$2.06	1	P	$206.00	$270.00
01/11/19	BO	03/15/19	$120.00	$1.58	1	P	-$162.00	108
02/20/19	BC	03/15/19	$124.00	$0.34	1	C	-$34.00	$74.00
02/20/19	SC	03/15/19	$129.00	$0.03	1	C	$3.00	$77.00
02/20/19	BC	03/15/19	$121.00	$0.65	1	P	-$69.00	$8.00
02/20/19	SC	03/15/19	$120.00	$0.33	1	P	$33.00	$41.00
							Profit of:	$41.00

XHB – 1/11/19 – Broken Wing Iron Condor

On 1/11 XHB was trading at $35.43 and I thought it was a good candidate for a broken wing iron condor with no downside risk. XHB looked to me like it had a much greater chance of heading down based on the chart pattern.

    I opened the trade with the 2/22/19 expiration options by selling the $36 Call, buying the $39 Call, selling the $36 Put and buying the $35 Put for a credit of $2.16. My risk on this trade was only $185.00 and it had a 74.52% chance of success. I was feeling really good about this on heading into the trade.

    I placed a GTC order to keep about 35% of the $2.16 opening credit.

    Things were going fine with this trade, time decay was doing its thing even though I was a little concerned about the price action. Then on 2/13 a massive up candle. Now I was in trouble.

    On 2/14 I started trying to adjust and kept trying right up until expiration on 2/22 but I could not find a way to adjust for a credit.

    On 2/22 with XHB trading at $39.08 I closed the Calls for a loss and just let the Puts expire worthless.

    I took right at max loss on this trade which is the way they work. After 42 days, I closed for a $181.00 loss or 97.84% based on risk. See, sometimes I do lose money too.

Date		EXP	Strike	Price	Ct	C/P	Cost	Balance
01/11/19	SO	02/22/19	$36.00	$0.84	1	C	$84.00	$84.00
01/11/19	BO	02/22/19	$39.00	$0.11	1	C	-$11.00	$73.00
01/11/19	SO	02/22/19	$36.00	$1.43	1	P	$143.00	$216.00
01/11/19	BO	02/22/19	$35.00	$0.97	1	P	-$101.00	115
02/22/19	BC	02/22/19	$36.00	$3.11	1	C	-$313.00	-$198.00
02/22/19	SC	02/22/19	$39.00	$0.17	1	C	$17.00	-$181.00
							Loss of:	-$181.00

V – 1/31/19 – Broken Wing Iron Condor

I actually placed this trade as a hedge on a diagonal I have been fighting for what seems like a year. This was a good trade in its own right.

On 1/31 with V trading at $135.27 I entered into a broken wing iron condor that had an initial probability of success of about 68.66%. Implied volatility was at 19.78 which was not great but for V it OK. The chart showed good upward momentum and support below by downside break even. I don't place these trades based on chart patterns but they are good for confirmation.

I used the 3/22/19 expiration options. I sold the $133 Call and bought the $134 Call. I sold the $132 Put and bought the $127 Put for a credit of $1.80 to finish up my broken wing iron condor. I set a GTC for $1.22.

On 2/11 I decided to close the trade at $1.25 for a profit of $47.00 or 14.51% on my risk after 12 days. The main reason I close was V was trading at $142.40 and I was stuck at that profit level. Since I did not expect a move down anytime soon it just made more since to close for close to target profit that wait another 30 days for a small amount more.

Date		EXP	Strike	Price	Ct	C/P	Cost	Balance
01/31/19	SO	03/22/19	$133.00	$5.80	1	C	$580.00	$580.00
01/31/19	BO	03/22/19	$134.00	$4.82	1	C	-$482.00	$98.00
01/31/19	SO	03/22/19	$132.00	$2.51	1	P	$251.00	$349.00
01/31/19	BO	03/22/19	$127.00	$1.69	1	P	-$173.00	176
02/12/19	BC	03/22/19	$133.00	$10.47	1	C	-$1,047.00	-$871.00
02/12/19	SC	03/22/19	$134.00	$9.59	1	C	$959.00	$88.00

02/12/19	B C	03/22/19	$132.00	$0.76	1	P	-$80.00	$8.00
02/12/19	S C	03/22/19	$127.00	$0.39	1	P	$39.00	$47.00
							Profit of:	$47.00

Chapter 5

Butterflys

I have been trading Butterfly's more lately but they can be difficult to manage if you spend to much to get into one. Also, if you are using a trade calculator showing your maximum profit remember that is if you hold the position until expiration and it finishes at exactly the price of your short. That rarely happens. I usually close butterfly's early for a reasonable return. What is reasonable? Depends on what you paid to get into it. I try to limit my risk, so I shoot for a higher percentage return. However, that may only be half what the potential was.

Pay attention, there is a difference when you sell or buy a butterfly. When you sell them your probably of success if you set them up right should be MUCH greater, but your return will be a lot lower.

By comparison when you buy a butterfly you will usually spend less money (less risk) which means better returns but your probability of success is MUCH lower.

We typically sell butterflys as part of our overall trading strategy but every once in a while you will find us on the buyer side.

The older trades show the actual contracts we traded. The newer ones I defaulted to 1 or 2 contracts because I wanted to make you focus more on the actual trade not the net profit. It is the percentages we want to focus on.

In my first Watch me Trade book, which the older trades are out of I used actual contracts, in my Watch me Trade 2 I shifted to a default number of contracts for the reason above regardless of how many I really traded in my account.

RCL – 07/05/2016 – Butterfly

I entered this trade based on a weekly candle, I felt there was some upward potential for this stock. With RCL trading at $68.06 I bought five AUG16 $70 Calls, sold ten AUG16 $72.50 Calls and purchased five AUG16 $75 Calls to form my Butterfly. Ideally, I wanted this stock to close right at $72.50 or reach it at some point that I could exit the trade with a profit.

By 7/12 RCL had moved up to $72.17 but the position was still showing a loss, probably because of how much time was left on the options. On 7/25 it had moved up to $73.06 and still showing a loss, this was disappointing to me and another reason I do not like Butterflys.

On 8/2 the bottom had fallen out and RCL was trading at $67.51, fortunately I was only showing a small loss which was somewhat of a surprise to me initially until I took into effect that volatility had increased actually helping my option prices. On 8/5 RCL had recovered to $73.97 and I was able to exit the position with a nice return. My risk on this trade was only $132.50, the price to purchase the Butterfly. I ended up with a profit of $46.65 or 35.21% on 31 days. Annualized at 414%. Good return, but I did not like the way the options performed.

Date		Exp	Strike	Price	Ct	C/P	Cost	Balance
07/05/16	BO	AUG16	70	-$2.43	5	C	-$1,217.50	-$1,217.50
07/05/16	SO	AUG16	72.5	$1.58	10	C	$1,580.00	$362.50
07/05/16	BO	AUG16	75	-$0.99	5	C	-$495.00	-$132.50
08/05/16	SC	AUG16	70	$4.30	5	C	$572.27	$439.77
08/05/16	BC	AUG16	72.5	-$2.53	10	C	-$2,535.41	-$2,095.64
08/05/16	SC	AUG16	75	$1.15	5	C	$2,142.29	$46.65

NOTE: This butterfly would have performed better if I had

a larger range. Just a $5.00 range was not big enough for this trade. But that would have also cost more.

NKE – 9/12/18 – Butterfly

We sold this Butterfly on 9/12 with Implied Volatility at 72 and earnings scheduled for 9/25. Since we were short we wanted a big move away from our entry point.

With NKE trading at $82.44 we sold the 10/19 $77.50 Call, bought the $82.50 Call and sold the $87.50 Call. Our max loss would be $723.00 if NKE expired right at $82.50. Our max potential gain was $276.00

This trade DID NOT move like we wanted through earnings, at one point we were down over $250.00, but on 10/10 we got lucky and NKE had a major down day which triggered our GTC order. I say luck but we also had probability on our side, still you never know with the market.

We closed with a profit of $76.00 after 28 days or 10.51%. Your return is lower when you sell a Butterfly as opposed to buying one but your probability of success is usually MUCH higher.

Date		EXP	Strike	Price	Ct	C/P	Cost	Balance
09/12/18	SO	10/19/18	$77.50	$6.15	2	C	$1,230.00	$1,230.00
09/12/18	BO	10/19/18	$82.50	$2.91	4	C	-$1,164.00	$66.00
09/12/18	SO	10/19/18	$87.50	$1.05	2	C	210	$276.00
10/08/18	BC	10/19/18	$77.50	$1.20	2	C	-$240.00	$36.00
10/08/18	SC	10/19/18	$82.50	$0.11	4	C	$44.00	$80.00
10/08/18	BC	10/19/18	$87.50	$0.02	2	C	-$4.00	$76.00
							Profit of:	$76.00

DIS – 9/19/18 – Butterfly

We were playing with the ThinkorSwim spread hacker and found this Butterfly that we could sell. It had an initial probability of success 72.76% although we felt the Implied Volatility was a little on the low side.

On 9/19 DIS was trading at $110.00 so we sold the 10/26 $112.00 Call, bought the $117.00 Call and sold the $122.00 Call for a credit of $.85. Our max risk on this trade if it expired right at $117.00 was $414.31 with a potential profit of $85.00.

Let me start by saying we did something wrong here. Our long Call was at $117.00 instead of $110.00 which is what DIS was at when we entered the trade. If we had entered this trade like normal we would have made money. However we basically said we think DIS is going to stay the same or move down, instead of just move.

DIS proceeded to move right up to our max loss position and even through it. On 10/10 we were showing a $117.00 loss with DIS trading at $115.55.

On 10/19 with a week left until expiration DIS was trading at $118.51 and we were getting concerned about a max loss based on the chart and no reason to expect a move over $122.00 or below $112.00. Therefore we decided to close and take the loss we had right now.

We closed for a $166.00 loss over 30 days or -40.77%. If we had traded this like we normally trade a Butterfly we actually would have made money. Sometimes we still outsmart ourselves.

Date		EXP	Strike	Price	Ct	C/P	Cost	Balance
09/19/18	SO	10/26/18	$112.00	$1.45	1	C	$145.00	$145.00
09/19/18	BO	10/26/18	$117.00	$0.35	2	C	-$70.00	$75.00
09/19/18	SO	10/26/18	$122.00	$0.10	1	C	$10.00	$85.00
10/19/18	BC	10/26/18	$112.00	$4.40	1	C	-$440.00	-$355.00

10/19/18	SC	10/26/18	$117.00	$0.98	2	C	$196.00	-$159.00
10/19/18	BC	10/26/18	$122.00	$0.07	1	C	-$7.00	-$166.00
							Loss of:	-$166.00

XRT – 9/20/18 – Butterfly

I bought an XRT butterfly on 9/20 despite Implied Volatility being much higher than I would have preferred. This was one of those 'gut' feeling trades that I do from time to time. Of course, it being a high potential return with only about 8 days until expiration helped make it worth the risk for me.

With XRT trading at $51.59 I bought the 9/28 $50.50 Call, sold the $51.50 Call and bought the $52.00 Call. Notice my spread was not the same between my Calls, not a typical butterfly.

My max loss here was my debit of $147.00, max profit would be $152.00 if it expired right at $51.50 (my short Calls).

I set my GTC order a $.75 credit which hit on 9/28 keeping about half my potential profit. I finished with a profit of $78.00 over 8 days or 53.06%. XRT was trading at $51.53 when my GTC order was hit. I might have been able to make more if I had held but that is not the way I trade.

Date		EXP	Strike	Price	Ct	C/P	Cost	Balance
09/20/18	BO	09/28/18	$50.50	$1.21	3	C	-$363.00	-$363.00
09/20/18	SO	09/28/18	$51.50	$0.49	6	C	$294.00	-$69.00
09/20/18	BO	09/28/18	$52.00	$0.26	3	C	-$78.00	-$147.00
09/28/18	SC	09/28/18	$50.50	$1.05	3	C	$315.00	$168.00
09/28/18	BC	09/28/18	$51.50	$0.17	6	C	-$102.00	$66.00
09/28/18	S	09/28/18	$52.00	$0.04	3	C	$12.00	$78.00

	C						
						Profit of:	$78.00

AGN – 09/20/18 – Butterfly

AGN had a very low Implied Volatility as I analyzed this trade. It had been in a very tight channel over the past 30 days so it looked like a good opportunity to purchase a Butterfly with a short expiration.

With AGN trading at $190.37 I bought the 9/28 $187.50 Calls, sold the $190.00 Calls and bought the $192.50 Calls. My risk on this trade was only $96.00 with a potential profit of $375.00 if AGN was trading exactly at $190.00 on 9/28. I set my GTC order to try and make about $95.00 on this trade.

Break even at expiration was $188.00 and $192.00.

On 9/26 AGN was trading at $188.16 and my GTC order hit. This time I was glad to have a modest GTC order out there as the price was moving toward my break even point and Implied Volatility was actually spiking up. Time decay did the trick and I closed for a profit.

I made $104.00 over 6 days on a risk of $96.00 or 108.33%. This was a good trade, although I could have just as easily lost the $96.00. When you see great returns like these it means there is a large risk of failure, that is why you get the returns. We look at these very carefully.

Date		EXP	Strike	Price	Ct	C/P	Cost	Balance
09/20/18	BO	09/28/18	$187.50	$4.00	2	C	-$800.00	-$800.00
09/20/18	SO	09/28/18	$190.00	$2.38	4	C	$952.00	$152.00
09/20/18	BO	09/28/18	$192.50	$1.24	2	C	-$248.00	-$96.00
09/26/18	SC	09/28/18	$187.50	$2.01	2	C	$402.00	$306.00
09/26/18	BC	09/28/18	$190.00	$0.79	4	C	-$316.00	-$10.00

09/26/18	SC	09/28/18	$192.50	$0.57	2	C	$114.00	$104.00
							Profit of:	$104.00

MU – 9/21/18 – Butterfly

On 9/12 with MU trading at $42.06 we decided to short a Butterfly with earnings coming up on 9/20. MU's Implied Volatility was at 80 and we started with a max profit potential of $260.00 on a risk of $738.00.

We started out with a $1.30 credit and placed a $.70 GTC order at the same time. To be profitable at expiration we needed MU to trade below $36.32 or above $43.70. Our maximum loss would be at $39.80.

On 9/18 our trade was up $45.00 with MU already up to $45.75 with earnings coming out on 9/20.

On 9/20 MU was trading at $46.28 before the earnings announcement. We decided we had more risk to hold through earnings than to close for a profit of $50.00 right now. So, we closed and took the profit.

We closed this trade after 8 days for a profit of $50.00 or 6.78%

Date		EXP	Strike	Price	Ct	C/P	Cost	Balance
09/12/18	SO	10/26/18	$35.00	$7.50	2	C	$1,500.00	$1,500.00
09/12/18	BO	10/26/18	$40.00	$4.05	4	C	-$1,620.00	-$120.00
09/12/18	SO	10/26/18	$45.00	$1.90	2	C	$380.00	$260.00
09/20/18	BC	10/26/18	$35.00	$11.45	2	C	-$2,290.00	-$2,030.00
09/20/18	SC	10/26/18	$40.00	$7.05	4	C	$2,820.00	$790.00
09/20/18	BC	10/26/18	$45.00	$3.70	2	C	-$740.00	$50.00
							Profit of:	$50.00

MU – 10/9/18 – Butterfly

Our last trade in MU worked so we decided to try another one. Implied Volatility was fairly low which supported buying this trade and the risk was so low that it was almost a throw away trade, sometimes we do roll the dice.

Plus, it was a fairly short term trade which at least psychologically made us think the odds were better than they actually were. We felt that MU would gravitate toward the $42.50 level over the next week or so.

With MU trading at $42.18 we bought the 10/19 $41.00 Calls, sold the $42.50 Calls and bought the $44.00 Calls. Our max profit was about $241.00 if MU finished right at $42.50 with a total risk of $58.00. We set a GTC for about a $120.00 profit and waited to see.

On 10/16, three days before expiration MU had moved back to $42.52 but our profit was still not at the $120.00 level. We decided to try and work on a close for this one and just get as much as we could.

On 10/17 with MU at $42.74 we closed this trade for a $60.00 profit over 8 days for a 103.45% return. Not too bad.

Date		EXP	Strike	Price	Ct	C/P	Cost	Balance
10/09/18	BO	10/19/18	$41.00	$1.95	2	C	-$390.00	-$390.00
10/09/18	SO	10/19/18	$42.50	$1.09	4	C	$436.00	$46.00
10/09/18	BO	10/19/18	$44.00	$0.52	2	C	-$104.00	-$58.00
10/17/18	SC	10/19/18	$41.00	$1.78	2	C	$356.00	$298.00
10/17/18	BC	10/19/18	$42.50	$0.67	4	C	-$268.00	$30.00
10/17/18	SC	10/19/18	$44.00	$0.15	2	C	$30.00	$60.00
							Profit of:	$60.00

MU – 1/17/19 – Butterfly

I decided to short a MU butterfly with MU trading at $33.44 I sold the 3/15/19 expiration $31.00 Call, bought the $34.00 Call and sold the $37.00 Call to complete the short butterfly.

I sold the trade for a credit of $.60 and set a GTC for $.30. There were no earnings but I still though MU would move.

On 1/25 MU gapped up to $37.86 and my GTC hit.

I finished the trade with a profit of $54.00 or 11.32% in just 8 days. Perfect short Butterfly.

Date		EXP	Strike	Price	Ct	C/P	Cost	Balance
01/17/19	SO	03/15/19	$31.00	$3.95	2	C	$790.00	$790.00
01/17/19	BO	03/15/19	$34.00	$2.23	4	C	-$900.00	-$110.00
01/17/19	SO	03/15/19	$37.00	$1.11	2	C	$222.00	$112.00
01/25/19	BC	03/15/19	$31.00	$7.75	2	C	-$1,550.00	-$1,438.00
01/25/19	SC	03/15/19	$34.00	$5.35	4	C	$2,140.00	$702.00
01/25/19	BC	03/15/19	$37.00	$3.20	2	C	-$648.00	$54.00
							Profit of:	$54.00

IBM – 1/17/19 – Butterfly

On 1/17 with IBM trading at $121.30 I decided to short a butterfly by selling the 3/15/19 expiration $115.00 call, buying the $120.00 call and selling the $125.00 call. I got a credit of $.86 and set a GTC order for $.43.

On 1/23 IBM had a major spike up to $131.37 because of

earnings and my GTC order hit. I closed the trade for a profit of $144.00 or 17.60% in just 6 days.

Date		EXP	Strike	Price	Ct	C/P	Cost	Balance
01/17/19	SO	03/15/19	$115.00	$9.05	2	C	$1,810.00	$1,810.00
01/17/19	BO	03/15/19	$120.00	$5.60	4	C	-$2,248.00	-$438.00
01/17/19	SO	03/15/19	$125.00	$3.05	2	C	$610.00	$172.00
01/23/19	BC	03/15/19	$115.00	$16.70	2	C	-$3,340.00	-$3,168.00
01/23/19	SC	03/15/19	$120.00	$11.80	4	C	$4,720.00	$1,552.00
01/23/19	BC	03/15/19	$125.00	$7.00	2	C	-$1,408.00	$144.00
							Profit of:	$144.00

SPX – 1/18/19 – Butterfly

On 1/18 I decided to short an SPX butterfly using the 3/15 expiration options. I sold the $2640 call, bought the $2670 call, and sold the $2700 call for a $2.80 credit. I set my GTC order at $1.40.

SPX was trading at $2673.00 when I entered the trade and I was showing a probability of success of 87.34%, which is why I took this trade.

The next day, SPX moved down to $2665.18 and my GTC order hit. I was able to get a 5.56% profit in just a day.

Date		EXP	Strike	Price	Ct	C/P	Cost	Balance
01/18/19	SO	03/15/19	$2,640.00	$82.70	1	C	$8,270.00	$8,270.00
01/18/19	BO	03/15/19	$2,670.00	$63.70	2	C	-$12,744.00	-$4,474.00
01/18/19	SO	03/15/19	$2,700.00	$47.50	1	C	$4,750.00	$276.00

Date		EXP	Strike	Price	Ct	C/P	Cost	Balance
01/19/19	BC	03/15/19	$2,640.00	$78.50	1	C	-$7,850.00	-$7,574.00
01/19/19	SC	03/15/19	$2,670.00	$60.80	2	C	$12,160.00	$4,586.00
01/19/19	BC	03/15/19	$2,700.00	$44.40	1	C	-$4,444.00	$142.00
							Profit of:	$142.00

FB – 1/23/19 – Butterfly

On 1/23 with FB trading at $144.12 I decided to enter into a short butterfly based on our swing trade indicator, earnings coming out in a week and high implied volatility.

We sold the 3/15 expiration $135 call, bought the $145 call and sold the $155 call to complete our short butterfly for a credit of $1.86. I set our GTC for $.90 and waited.

On 1/31 FB shot up to $166.25 after earnings and our GTC was hit closing the trade for a $132.00 profit after 8 days. A 16.22% return!

Date		EXP	Strike	Price	Ct	C/P	Cost	Balance
01/23/19	SO	03/15/19	$135.00	$13.85	1	C	$1,385.00	$1,385.00
01/23/19	BO	03/15/19	$145.00	$7.85	2	C	-$1,574.00	-$189.00
01/23/19	SO	03/15/19	$155.00	$3.75	1	C	$375.00	$186.00
01/31/19	BC	03/15/19	$135.00	$33.70	1	C	-$3,370.00	-$3,184.00
01/31/19	SC	03/15/19	$145.00	$24.00	2	C	$4,800.00	$1,616.00
01/31/19	BC	03/15/19	$155.00	$14.80	1	C	-$1,484.00	$132.00
							Profit of:	$132.00

TSLA – 1/24/19 – Butterfly

TSLA was trading at $285.56 with a high implied volatility. The probability of success when I entered this trade was 88.25%. TSLA can be hard to trade because the option prices can vary greatly each day because of the bid/ask spread. This time it worked to our advantage.

We sold the 3/15 expiration short butterfly by selling the $270 call, buying the $285 call and selling the $300 call for a credit of $1.31. We then set our GTC order for about $.65 and waited.

This time we did not have to wait long, the trade closed in one day because of the bid/ask spreads and a change in implied volatility.

We closed the trade for a $77.00 profit in a day which was a 5.62% return.

TSLA is actually hard to trade sometimes, so we don't trade it that often.

Date	EXP	Strike	Price	Ct	C/P	Cost	Balance
01/24/19	SO 03/15/19	$270.00	$37.35	1	C	$3,735.00	$3,735.00
01/24/19	BO 03/15/19	$285.00	$28.65	2	C	-$5,734.00	-$1,999.00
01/24/19	SO 03/15/19	$300.00	$21.30	1	C	$2,130.00	$131.00
01/25/19	BC 03/15/19	$270.00	$40.30	1	C	-$4,030.00	-$3,899.00
01/25/19	SC 03/15/19	$285.00	$31.75	2	C	$6,350.00	$2,451.00
01/25/19	BC 03/15/19	$300.00	$23.70	1	C	-$2,374.00	$77.00
						Profit of:	$77.00

CMG – 1/24/19 – Butterfly

On 1/24 CMG was trading at $524.60 with earnings coming out on 2/6. We decided to short a butterfly by selling the 3/15/19 expiration $500 call, buying the $520 call and selling the $540 call for a credit of $2.06. We set our GTC for $1.03.

The next day our GTC hit as the CMG price fluctuated and implied volatility dropped down from the 76.11 we entered at.

We were able to close this trade after a day for a profit of $132.00 or about 7.36%. Not too bad, but like TSLA, CMG can be hard to manage. We had a good deal of luck with the spreads.

Date		EXP	Strike	Price	Ct	C/P	Cost	Balance
01/24/19	SO	03/15/19	$500.00	$45.30	1	C	$4,530.00	$4,530.00
01/24/19	BO	03/15/19	$520.00	$33.60	2	C	-$6,724.00	-$2,194.00
01/24/19	SO	03/15/19	$540.00	$24.00	1	C	$2,400.00	$206.00
01/25/19	BC	03/15/19	$500.00	$45.50	1	C	-$4,550.00	-$4,344.00
01/25/19	SC	03/15/19	$520.00	$34.40	2	C	$6,880.00	$2,536.00
01/25/19	BC	03/15/19	$540.00	$24.00	1	C	-$2,404.00	$132.00
							Profit of:	$132.00

AAPL – 1/24/19 – Butterfly

With AAPL trading at $153.51 and earnings coming out on 1/29 we decided to place a short butterfly using the 3/15/19 expiration options. We sold the $145 call, bought the $155 call and sold the $165 call for a credit of $2.24. We set our GTC at $1.12.

We had a 71.82% probability of success going into this trade.

On 2/5 AAPL spiked up to $173.15 and our GTC was hit. We closed for a profit of $110.00 in 12 days or 14.07%.

Date		EXP	Strike	Price	Ct	C/P	Cost	Balance
01/24/19	SO	03/15/19	$145.00	$11.60	1	C	$1,160.00	$1,160.00
01/24/19	BO	03/15/19	$155.00	$5.75	2	C	-$1,154.00	$6.00

01/24/19	SO	03/15/19	$165.00	$2.18	1	C	$218.00	$224.00
02/05/19	BC	03/15/19	$145.00	$27.90	1	C	-$2,790.00	-$2,566.00
02/05/19	SC	03/15/19	$155.00	$18.20	2	C	$3,640.00	$1,074.00
02/05/19	BC	03/15/19	$165.00	$9.60	1	C	-$964.00	$110.00
							Profit of:	$110.00

CMG – 1/25/19 – Butterfly

On 1/25 CMG had just broke to a new 52 week high and it had earnings coming out on 2/6. With implied volatility at 73.96 we really felt like CMG was set up for good move which would make a short butterfly a good option strategy to use.

Using the 3/15/19 expiration options we sold the $520 call, bought the $540 call and sold the $560 call for a credit of $2.06. We set our GTC at $1.05.

On 2/6 our GTC hit as CMG dropped to $524.55. We closed the trade for a profit of $162.00 after 12 days or 9.03%.

Date		EXP	Strike	Price	Ct	C/P	Cost	Balance
01/25/19	SO	03/15/19	$520.00	$43.90	1	C	$4,390.00	$4,390.00
01/25/19	BO	03/15/19	$540.00	$32.40	2	C	-$6,484.00	-$2,094.00
01/25/19	SO	03/15/19	$560.00	$23.00	1	C	$2,300.00	$206.00
02/06/19	BC	03/15/19	$520.00	$29.80	1	C	-$2,980.00	-$2,774.00
02/06/19	SC	03/15/19	$540.00	$21.60	2	C	$4,320.00	$1,546.00
02/06/19	BC	03/15/19	$560.00	$13.80	1	C	-$1,384.00	$162.00
							Profit of:	$162.00

GILD – 1/31/19 – Butterfly

On 1/31 GILD was trading at $69.44 and had earnings scheduled for 2/4. It had been in a channel for a while so I was a little worried, but I felt that if earnings give it that momentum it needed to break out of the channel this could be a really good trade.

I sold the 3/15 expiration $65 call, bought the $70 call and sold the $75 call for a $1.44 credit to get into my short butterfly. I set a GTC for about $.72 and waited.

On 2/6 a couple of days after earnings I was not seeing the movement I had hoped for. GILD was trading at $64.53 but I was afraid it was going to move back up toward $70.00 which would be bad for my short butterfly so I closed for a small profit.

I ended up making $31.00 or about 8.61% over 12 days. Sometimes you have to take what is there after earnings.

Date		EXP	Strike	Price	Ct	C/P	Cost	Balance
01/31/19	SO	03/15/19	$65.00	$5.60	1	C	$560.00	$560.00
01/31/19	BO	03/15/19	$70.00	$2.52	2	C	-$508.00	$52.00
01/31/19	SO	03/15/19	$75.00	$0.88	1	C	$88.00	$140.00
02/12/19	BC	03/15/19	$65.00	$1.61	1	C	-$161.00	-$21.00
02/12/19	SC	03/15/19	$70.00	$0.33	2	C	$66.00	$45.00
02/12/19	BC	03/15/19	$75.00	$0.10	1	C	-$14.00	$31.00
							Profit of:	$31.00

QCOM – 1/25/2019 – Butterfly

This trade had a nice potential risk verses reward when I entered it. I could make as much as $266.00 on a risk of $238.00 all with a 74.42% probability of success.

There was an issue when I entered the trade, I could not get the correct strikes because they were not offered. I ended up with more risk on the downside which is not a true butterfly. Also one reason the risk/reward was skewed.

With QCOM trading at $51.43 I sold the 3/15/19 $45 call, bought the $50 call and sold the $52.50 call for a credit of $2.66. Because I got such a good credit I put my GTC order at $1.80.

Earnings were coming out on 1/30 so I really felt good about this trade.

On 2/1 there was almost no move after earnings. I decided to stay in the trade since it still had a lot of time left.

By 2/19 there was less than 30 days left on the trade and QCOM was not moving at all. In fact, I was really concerned it would make a move down and put me in a worse position.

With QCOM trading at $51.95 I decided to close for a $51.00 loss or 21.43% on my risk over 25 days. I still think this was a good trade to enter, it just did not work out. That happens sometimes.

Date		EXP	Strike	Price	Ct	C/P	Cost	Balance
01/25/19	SO	03/15/19	$45.00	$7.05	1	C	$705.00	$705.00
01/25/19	BO	03/15/19	$50.00	$3.15	2	C	-$634.00	$71.00
01/25/19	SO	03/15/19	$52.50	$1.91	1	C	$191.00	$262.00
02/19/19	BC	03/15/19	$45.00	$7.00	1	C	-$700.00	-$438.00
02/19/19	SC	03/15/19	$50.00	$2.45	2	C	$490.00	$52.00
02/19/19	BC	03/15/19	$52.50	$0.99	1	C	-$103.00	-$51.00
							Profit of:	-$51.00

WMT – 2/19/19 – Butterfly

WMT had earnings on 2/18 after market close, I had missed it. Should have shorted a butterfly before earnings. However, WMT had such a gap and run up I decided to take a chance and jump in after the release.

With WMT trading at $103.07 I sold the 3/29 $99.50 Call, bought the $103.00 Call and sold the $106.00 Call for $1.13 go get into my short butterfly. I put in a GTC order for $.55 after I got filled.

We actually got the move we expected in WMT. The problem was it started right after we entered the traded. In 2 days WMT had closed the gap and retraced to a previous support level. With WMT trading at $99.55 and finding support we were then worried WMT would continue is previous trend and slowly make its way back to the midpoint of our short butterfly at $103.00 which would be worst case for us.

Therefore, even though we got the move we wanted, we felt we had to close this trade for a much smaller profit. We closed for a profit of 6.64% in just two days. WMT just made its move too fast.

Date		EXP	Strike	Price	Ct	C/P	Cost	Balance
02/19/19	SO	03/29/19	$99.50	$5.10	1	C	$510.00	$510.00
02/19/19	BO	03/29/19	$103.00	$2.58	2	C	-$520.00	-$10.00
02/19/19	SO	03/29/19	$106.00	$1.19	1	C	$119.00	$109.00
02/21/19	BC	03/29/19	$99.50	$2.01	1	C	-$201.00	-$92.00
02/21/19	SC	03/29/19	$103.00	$0.66	2	C	$132.00	$40.00
02/21/19	BC	03/29/19	$106.00	$0.20	1	C	-$24.00	$16.00
							Profit of:	$16.00

Chapter 6

Strangles

Strangles are the only uncapped risk, limited reward strategy we trade. As a result we are highly selective about how we trade Strangles.

We base our strangle trades like we place our probability based non-index and Broken Wing Iron Condors. We use probabilities and volatility. In addition because these are uncapped risk we typically only trade stocks that have predictable moves. We stay away from stocks that might have sudden earnings like pharmaceuticals. We also try to have only one stock from a particular industry in our Strangle portfolio at a given time, just in case something affects that entire industry.

Some stocks that we like for Strangles at the time we are writing this are: MSFT, DIS, MCD, NKE, CAT, MU and others. This is not meant as a complete list, only to give you an idea of what we are looking for.

If you do not know what a Strangle is, let's dive into that first. First of all, we typically only short Strangles, that is why we said we have unlimited risk and capped profit potential. If you buy a Strangle it is the opposite but we rarely do that. We have found shorting Strangles to have a higher success rate if done correctly. Or at least following a set of rules we have worked on over the years.

A short Strangle, the way we trade them, consists of selling a out of the money (OTM) Call and an OTM Put against a security. Your potential profit is the credit you received for placing the Strangle and your potential risk is unlimited to the upside and the stock price down to $0.00 to the downside. For all practical purposes we call that unlimited on both sides.

Perhaps it is easier to give you an example at this point.

We recently shorted a Strangle in MCD.

With MCD trading at $179.16 we sold a Strangle which expires in 45 days. We sold the $187.50 Call and the $170.00 Put for a credit of $2.02 or $202.00 per contract. Our overall risk is unlimited but the effect on our buying power is $2,750.00. Buying power effect can vary depending on a number of factors. If we held to close our return would be 7.3%

As soon as we placed the trade we placed at Good to Cancel (GTC) order for $1.65 meaning we are going to try and make $37.00 per contract on this trade. If our GTC order hits we make about 1.3% on this trade. I know that does not sound like much but this is a very high probability trade. In addition our average time in a Strangle is about 10 days as we are writing this.

This means we could theoretically get a 1.3% return every 10 days if nothing goes wrong. Annualized that would be about 47.45% return on buying power used.

So, what are the short Strangle rules we use (most of the time)?

1. Use high quality, somewhat predictable stocks. You do not want a stock with a history of large random movements.

2. Higher volatility improves your chances of success. Here we are referring to a higher volatility for the stock you are trading not overall volatility. A pharmaceutical might have a much larger volatility but we are only concerned where our stock is as compared to historical volatility.

3. Try for a potential initial return of about 10% as long as it has a probability of success over 65%.

4. Look to close for around a 3% return or about 35% of your initial credit. So if your initial credit was $2.00 then you would consider closing at $1.30 giving you a $.70 profit.

5. Try to get a probability of over 65%. We use the TDAmeritrade platform to give us probabilities, you could use Delta's and Volatility to calculate but that is more than we are getting into here.

6. Try to find short Calls and Puts that are at support and

resistance points. Use the chart and see what looks like a good place to put your Calls and Puts. If one of them appears to be in the middle of a price action zone the find another security to trade. You do not have to be a chart or trend line expert, just use your eyes.

      7.   Stay away from stocks with earnings or other expected news events before you Strangle expires is you are shorting Strangles, the opposite applies if you are long a Strangle.

      8.   DO NOT over trade them. These types of trades make up about 10% of our portfolio at any given time. Remember, uncapped risk.

Adjustment Rules. Again, these are the ones we try to follow. But, you have to decide for yourself where you need to adjust.

      1.   If the loss on the trade is showing more that twice what you are trying to make. In the MCD trade above since we are trying to make $37.00 if the trade ever shows a $74.00 loss we need to look at it.

      2.   If the price of the underlying security is approaching one of your short options.

      3.   If you have to adjust try to close the trade at just above break even. The security has already moved against you, it might be best to just get out as soon as you can and move to the next trade.

How to Adjust.

      1.   You can always just close the trade for a loss or small profit.

      2.   You can roll the Strangle out another week or more. Only do this if you can do it for a credit AND it places your new short positions at a strong resistance or support level.

Here is an example of a Strangle we had to adjust.

We placed a trade in NKE with about 45 days to expiration. NKE was trading at $80.10 when we placed the trade by selling the

$85.00 Call and the $75.00 Put.

Fourteen days later NKE was trading at $85.15, because of time decay and the loss of value in our short Put we were not showing a loss of twice what we were trying to make. So, instead of closing we decided to look for a roll.

Our initial break even to the upside was $86.64 (our short call plus the $1.64 credit we received when we placed the trade) which was right at the 52 week high.

We found a roll that pushed the trade out another week and brought in an additional $.34 credit. So, we rolled the trade from a short $75/$85 Strangle to a $79/$87.50 Strangle. With the move up in our short call and the additional credit we moved our break even point to the upside to $89.42, well above the 52 week high. Plus we did it by only adding a week to the trade.

Adjustments don't always work out this well. If the trade moves against you quickly or you can't improve your odds you are sometimes just better to close.

Below are some trades from our Trading Journal for review.

MU – 9/10/18 – Strangle

I used to trade MU a lot, just getting back into the swing of things with this security. I decided to take advantage of some sideways movement and good premium in the market.

This trade started out with about a 80% probability of success based on the strikes I chose and current movement in the security. I entered the trade selling the 10/26/18 $55.00 Call and the 10/26/18 $35.00 Put with MU trading at $45.04 for a total premium for $1.18.

I made a mistake when entering this trade, not realizing that MU had earnings on 9/20. Something you have to remember to check. So, I started watching for a quicker opportunity to exit than normal. Found the opportunity for a quick profit the next day.

Ended up with a $36.00 profit on a risk of $1,136.00 or about 3.17%. That doesn't sound great but I REALLY wanted out and if you annualized this it was about 1156.69%

Date	EXP	Strike	Price	Ct	C/P	Cost	Balance
09/10/18	SO 10/26/18	$55.00	$.76	2	C	$152.00	$152.00
09/10/18	SO 10/26/18	$35.00	$.42	2	P	$84.00	$236.00
09/11/18	BC 10/26/18	$55.00	$.51	2	C	-$102.00	$134.00
09/11/18	BC 10/26/18	$35.00	$.49	2	P	-$98.00	$36.00
						Profit of:	$36.00

MS – 09/13/18 - Strangle

MS had been in a downward trend but was still moving in a somewhat predictable fashion, so I decided to place a Strangle on it.

MS was trading at $47.58 on 9/13 when I entered the position. I sold the 10/26/18 $50.00 Call and the $45.00 Put. The position was showing a probability of success of about 64% if held to expiration. The 52 week low as at $45.56 so I felt pretty good about my downside protection. I received a credit of $1.18 when I entered the trade and set a GTC at about $.90.

On 9/27/18 my GTC hit and I closed this position with a profit of $56.00 on a risk of $1450.00 or about 3.86%. Annualized at 100.69%. There was not much price movement as MS was trading at $47.77, however this sideways action caused the implied volatility to drop which enabled me to take advantage of time decay and a drop in implied volatility for a fairly quick profit.

Date	EXP	Strike	Price	Ct	C/P	Cost	Balance
09/13/18	SO 10/26/18	$50.00	$.61	2	C	$122.00	$122.00
09/13/18	SO 10/26/18	$45.00	$.57	2	P	$114.00	$236.00

Date		EXP	Strike	Price	Ct	C/P	Cost	Balance
09/27/18	BC	10/26/18	$50.00	$.52	2	C	-$104.00	$132.00
09/27/18	BC	10/26/18	$45.00	$.38	2	P	-$76.00	$56.00
							Profit of:	$56.00

SMH – 10/19/18 – Strangle

On 10/19 SMH was trading at $95.37 and trading right at the 200 day moving average. I started looking at possible Strangle positions and was able to enter one that put by downside break even well below the 52 week low.

I sold the 11/23/18 $102.00 Call and the $90.00 Put for a credit of $2.34 with a probability of success at 64.4%. When I entered the trade the Implied Volatility was at 56.16. It actually went up by the time I exited to 72.35 but time decay and a move back toward my entry price enabled me to hit my GTC order.

On 11/1 the position automatically closed at $1.65 giving me a profit of $69.00 on a risk of $1,300.00 or about 5.31% which annualized at 149.02% over 13 days.

Date		EXP	Strike	Price	Ct	C/P	Cost	Balance
10/19/18	SO	11/23/18	$102.00	$1.07	1	C	$107.00	$107.00
10/19/18	SO	11/23/18	$90.00	$1.27	1	P	$127.00	$234.00
11/01/18	BC	11/23/18	$102.00	$.62	1	C	-$62.00	$172.00
11/01/18	BC	11/23/18	$90.00	$1.03	1	P	-$103.00	$69.00
							Profit of:	$69.00

DIS – 10/19/18 – Strangle

DIS is another one of my favorites for Strangles, I like how predictable it tends to trade. There was a little bit of added risk here because DIS had earnings on 11/8 and the expiration for this trade was 11/9. If I was not able to get out early this could be a problem. However, this time I was aware of the extra risk so I managed the trade accordingly.

On 10/19 with DIS trading at 118.61 and an implied volatility of 58.25 I sold the 11/9/18 $123.00 Call and the $114.00 Put for a total credit of $2.62. The trade was showing a 65.44% chance of success if held to expiration. I put in a GTC order for $1.99 hoping for a quick profit.

On 11/1 after 13 days my GTC order hit and I closed the position for a profit of $126.00 on a risk of $4,000.00 or 3.15%. Annualized this comes out to 88.44%

Date		EXP	Strike	Price	Ct	C/P	Cost	Balance
10/19/18	SO	11/09/18	$123.00	$.61	2	C	$122.00	$122.00
10/19/18	SO	11/09/18	$114.00	$2.01	2	P	$402.00	$524.00
11/01/18	BC	11/09/18	$123.00	$.23	2	C	-$46.00	$478.00
11/01/18	BC	11/09/18	$114.00	$1.76	2	P	-$352.00	$126.00
							Profit of:	$126.00

MSFT – 11/27/18 – Strangle

I like MSFT for Strangles because it moves in a predictable manner, most of the time anyway. Just as will all trades, watch out for earnings.

I entered this trade with MSFT trading at $106.12 and a implied volatility of 48.98. The probability of success if I held to expiration was about 69.34% when I entered, but of course I never plan on holding to expiration so my overall probability of success is somewhat higher.

I entered this trade on 11/27 by selling the 01/14/19 $117.00 Call and the $97.00 Put for a $1.51 credit. I set a GTC order at about

$0.94 to close this trade for a profit.

On 12/11/18 my GTC order was hit and I closed this trade after 14 days. I received a profit of $53.00 on a risk of $1,362.00 or about 3.89%. Annualized it was 101.45%

Date		EXP	Strike	Price	Ct	C/P	Cost	Balance
11/27/18	SO	1/14/19	$117.00	$.55	1	C	$54.00	$54.00
11/27/18	SO	01/14/19	$97.00	$.96	1	P	$95.00	$149.00
12/11/18	BC	01/14/19	$117.00	$.58	1	C	-$59.00	$90.00
12/11/18	BC	01/14/19	$97.00	$.36	1	P	-$37.00	$53.00
							Profit of:	$53.00

MSFT – 2/1/19

This trade went about perfect. When we entered the trade MSFT was trading at 103.54 and we sold the $97/$111 strangle with a probability of success of 68.36%. Implied volatility was at 22 when we entered ant 17.2 when we closed.

We started with a credit of $2.04 and put in a GTC order for $1.42. We ended up moving it up on 2/13 to $1.49 can manually closed the trade. We were just so close to our target we could not resist. Better to take the profit than the chance.

We where in the trade for 12 days and closed it for a 3.15% profit on a risk of $1,618.00. Annualized that is about 96% which is how we look at our short strangles.

Date		EXP	Strike	Price	Ct	C/P	Cost	Balance
02/01/19	SO	03/22/19	$111.00	$.77	1	C	$76.00	$76.00
02/01/19	SO	03/22/19	$97.00	$1.27	1	P	$126.00	$202.00

02/13/19	BC	03/22/19	$111.00	$1.09	1	C	-$109.00	$93.00
02/13/19	BC	03/22/19	$97.00	$0.40	1	P	-$42.00	$51.00
							Profit of:	$51.00

FB – 2/15/19

On 2/15 FB was trading at $161.48 with and implied volatility of about 31.56. I decided this was a good place to place a Strangle.

I sold the 3/29/19 $145 Put and the $180.00 Call for a credit of $1.71 and set a GTC order for $1.11. This trade was showing a 79.73% chance of success when I entered it.

On 2/22 after 7 days my GTC order hit and I made a profit of about $56.00 on a risk of $1,586.40 or about 3.53%.

Date		EXP	Strike	Price	Ct	C/P	Cost	Balance
02/15/19	SO	03/29/19	$180.00	0.63	1	C	$62.00	$62.00
02/15/19	SO	03/29/19	$145.00	$1.08	1	P	$107.00	$169.00
02/22/19	BC	03/29/19	$180.00	$0.34	1	C	-$36.00	$133.00
02/22/19	BC	03/29/19	$145.00	$0.77	1	P	-$77.00	$56.00
							Profit of:	$56.00

Conclusion/Take Away/Risk Warning

Trading is a risky business and there is risk of losing money. Trades and strategies that work today do not always work tomorrow. Market conditions change.

We have done our best to accurately present our trades here but there is always the possibility of errors. Do not think that just because one strategy or another is profitable for us that it will be profitable for you.

There are many factors that may not be represented here that go into our into our choosing one trade over another on any give day. We also did not include all of our trades, we tried to include a good variety of them that represented how we traded during the time period this book covers.

Looking at our past couple of years we were curious how successful we were in our trading. Keep in mind that none of these success rates are guaranteed to continue tomorrow, these are just a look into the past.

In 2016 our overall success rate was 65.52%

In 2017 our overall success rate was 66.67%

In 2018 our overall success rate was 71.11%

In 2019 we are focusing a lot more on the high probability range bound strategies so would expect our success rate to move up even more.

We track our success by some trade types and wanted to share them here as well. We do not have these broken down by year, some of the trades go back a number of years.

In Covered Calls and Diagonals over the years we are 81.63% successful.

In Index (SPX, RUT, NDX) based Iron Condors we are trading at 82.50%

In Index (SPX, RUT, QQQ) based Credit Spreads we are actually at 100%. This is an anomaly and there are not a lot of trades because we usually end up with these because we were not able to get good Iron Condor trades as we tried to leg into them. Another reason that these are at 100% is because typically the way we defend them is by turning them into an Iron Condor.

Probability based Iron Condors, Broken Wing Iron Condors and Strangles we are at 90.00% as of this writing.

Calendar trades are at 58.70%, which is not very good.

Butterfly trades are at 85.71%, these include both long and short butterflys but most of them are shorts.

Just a couple of words of advice that are really important.

1. Have a trading plan and stick to it.

2. Always know how and when you will adjust a trade before you enter it. Then DO IT! Don't wait, don't hope it will get better.

3. Be consistent.

4. Don't let fear or greed get you out of your trading plan.

I hope you have enjoyed and more importantly learned something reviewing my trades. To me, the only thing better than reviewing a persons trade journal is watching them trade during real market conditions. I do post more current trades on my website. Not usually in as much detail as in this book but after reading this you can probably determine my thinking on my ongoing trades.

I encourage you to check out my website, www.trade4profits.com, for lots more trading information and ongoing trades. Learning to trade profitably is not always easy, but it is easier if you have a community supporting you.

Check out our other books.

In Covered Calls – You are Doing it Wrong What if we told you everything you have been taught about writing Covered Calls is Wrong! What if we told you, you had been doing it wrong this entire time? Would you listen? Can we convince you there is a better way? If you can give us a short amount of your time we can show you how to get better returns, with less risk than writing your Grandfather's traditional Covered Call. There are so many better options (literally) than there used to be to a traditional Covered Call. Let us tell you about them.

If you have not read **Trade4Profits – Shortcuts to Profitable Trading** I urge you to do so. Shortcuts to Profitable trading will give you insights to many of the trades you have seen in this book. It will help you understand my basic trading philosophy and why I trade the way I do.

If you have not read **Trade4Profits – Watch Me Trade**, the one before this one. Then you should pick it up also. You will get to see some of the types of trades here. However, we were trading a little differently back then so you might learn something that is not in this book. You can decide which trading style you like best. There are some duplicate trades in this book and my Watch Me Trade book. There are some other types of trades which you might find interesting but about half the trades are in this book.

If you have not read **Trade4Profits – Watch Me Trade 2** it is a good read, but like my Watch Me Trade book there are a number of duplicate trades between this book and my Watch Me Trade 2 book. There are some other types of trades which you might find interesting but about half the trades are in this book.

I urge you to follow my twitter account at trade4profits1 to see what I am currently trading.

You can find a link to my books at www.trade4profits.com or www.jddawson.net

Good luck with your trading and don't forget to keep your own trading journal!

www.ingramcontent.com/pod-product-compliance
Lightning Source LLC
Chambersburg PA
CBHW030948240526
45463CB00016B/2168